PRAISE FOR *JOURNEYING* ...

"Tim Cavanagh writes a riveting and inspiring account of one man's plunge into the depths of the black hole of alcoholism, despair, and poor choices. This well-written account of his challenging climb upward is a must-read. Tim's story is an example of how disappointment, depression, and hopelessness can be overcome. This is a book that should be on everyone's bookshelf."

— **Helen Thayer**
Author of Polar Dream, Walking the Gobi, *and* Three Among the Wolves

"In this meticulously detailed and soulful account, Tim reveals his very personal journey: the childhood experiences that defined him, his strong-willed determination to fulfill his dreams, and the nightmarish tumble into disgrace and loss that launched him into a two-year program of self-discovery. His inspiring message to all of us is that—with disciplined intention, guided counseling, and the support of people who love us—it is possible to heal the wounded soul. Tim's touching story is proof."

— **Dr. Irene Simpson**
Doctor of Homeopathy, retired

JOURNEYING WELL
On Life's Rocky Trails

Journeying Well

On Life's Rocky Trails

———•◦✕◦•———

Dr. Tim Cavanagh

AnneMarie,

    May your trails be smooth
       and your mountains safe.

I appreciate your friendship
    and support all these years.

           Journey well,

              Tim

Published by Mountain Journey Center LLC,
Stanwood, Washington

Front cover photo by Tim Cavanagh
and author photo by Noel Imfeld.

Cover and interior book design by Mi Ae Lipe (whatnowdesign.com).

Printed in the United States of America.

To contact the author or order additional copies:
Dr. Tim Cavanagh
Mountain Journey Center LLC
26910 92nd Ave NW, Ste C5, PMB 211, Stanwood, WA 98292
journeyingwellrockytrails@gmail.com

First Edition, 2020
ISBN: 978-1-735-08620-0
Library of Congress Control Number: 2020916325

I dedicate this book to my children and grandchildren.
Without them the journey would not be worth the effort.

CONTENTS

Acknowledgments

I want to thank the many guides who have assisted me on my journey.

Legal Guides
>Lance (Criminal Case)
>Eric (Civil Lawsuit)

Emotional Guide
>Susan

Writing Guide
>Jennifer

Mountain Guides

Pete, Matias, David	(Mount Rainier 2019)
Andy, Grayson, Cal	(Glacier Peak 2019)
Hannah, Luke, Lucas	(Alaska 2019)
Eric, Jenny, Lydia, James, Nick	(Mount Rainier 2018)

THE TRAILHEAD

I have readied for this journey,
The best that I can.
I have prepared my provisions,
I have made my plans.

I awoke hours before dawn,
To set out on my quest.
I have picked a mountain,
That will prove a good test.

Over a curvy two-lane valley road,
In the early morning light.
I have traveled many miles,
Now the trailhead comes in sight.

At the base of the mountain,
My boots have not yet trod,
I know not what lies before me,
As the sun lights up the sod.

Always a bit of apprehension,
Is with me as I start,
But soon excitement overrides it,
And joy fills my heart.

I hope I am strong,
That I am up to the task.
I pray for a safe venture,
That is all I really ask.

I welcome the mountain's challenge,
Full of life's unknowns.
Into nature's beauty and bounty,
That is where I like to roam.

PROLOGUE

I started collecting moments of shame within myself when I was a little boy. I often suffered unjust punishment for the wrongs I did as a child until I felt the punishment did, indeed, fit the crime. I felt I was inherently bad. I found a special recess in my soul where I could store this badness; I started building my internal shame room. Each error I then committed throughout my life I added to this inner recess. Each time I drank too much, each time I was less-than-perfect, each time my woodworking had tiny flaws, and especially after my divorce, these dark moments accumulated to bursting until their dark shadows started to obscure the good light in my life.

The times of living in shame were frequently associated with my actions while I was drinking. It may have been something I said or did while drunk, or even just the fact that I got drunk when my intention was to only have two beers. My inability to control my drinking caused me shame. I would swear to do better, but failure was my constant companion. The area of my life most affected by this deep internal shame was in my relationships with women. I could not accept that a woman would just love me as the deeply flawed man I perceived myself to be.

These have been crippling emotions to carry.

After searching for a lifetime, I felt I had met the woman who completed me and with whom I thought I would spend the remainder of my life. I opened my heart to this woman, and I loved her dearly. I was as happy as I had been in years and I was filled with optimism at the end of 2015.

But New Year 2016 was not even two hours old before I saw through a window that Jim stood naked in Jodi's closet—the woman I dearly loved and had dreamed would be my wife. The shock of seeing this married man, whom Jodi had sworn was out of her life totally, was too much for me to handle.

One week later I was drunk and back at that same window in a reckless attempt to catch them together to force a confession of the truth. Instead of any satisfaction I might have garnered from hearing my beloved's confession, I was arrested for the first time in my life.

Less than two weeks later, my now-former girlfriend and her lover lay in wait for me to go to the monthly hospital board meeting that I had been attending for years. Unbeknownst to me, my presence on the hospital campus was a violation of the No Contact Order that had been imposed on me after my first arrest. Later that night, the cops arrived at my home and arrested me for the second time in my life.

Things were spiraling out of control. The emotional upheaval I felt was more than I could handle, and I turned to alcohol to assuage my shame. But all the booze did was to heap more pain on me as I slipped over the edge of my world. I got hopelessly drunk and drove around until I was pulled over and charged with a DUI, my first and only drunk driving offense. This was my third arrest in three weeks.

My world had imploded in the space of twenty-seven days. The year of 2016 would be bookended by institutions: February would find me in rehab for alcoholism and in mid-November I would be sent to jail for a month.

I had worked hard to keep others from seeing my shame and it was exhausting. It took all of my willpower to function and deal with normal life events. I had accumulated heaps of shame over my sixty years of living and now the dam that had held the shame within me broke. I collapsed into a seemingly irreparable mess.

GROWING UP

"I had a perfect childhood—we do not need to spend any time talking about it." These are the exact words I told Susan during the first five minutes of our introductory phone conversation that September 2014 day when I was searching for a therapist to help deal with the pain I was feeling over my first breakup with Jodi. Susan just acknowledged the statement, perhaps hearing denial in my words and voice even then. During that initial conversation with Susan, I felt she might be a good fit for me. We started weekly therapy sessions in October upon my return from Italy, a trip Jodi and I had planned to take prior to our breakup. Instead, I went alone.

I continued my story to Susan in that first therapy session. My dad had been strict, but he had needed to be with so many children. I described my mom as an angel who was always busy cooking, sewing, and keeping our house running. During the first two months, Susan would ask me questions about my childhood. I deflected them as I did not want to spend valuable time during our sessions discussing it. It had been a good childhood, not a source of problems or issues. I equated it to the families portrayed on *Leave It to Beaver* or *The Brady Bunch*. I loved my mom and dad, and I assumed that all families were like ours: with good and bad times. I chose to focus solely on the good times and built the image of my childhood based on those. This picture served as my rock and the foundation that helped me get through the difficult times of my life. This reexamination as an adult being guided by a therapist would lead me to change this image of perfection that I had carried with me for six decades.

I was born in Casper, Wyoming, on August 25, 1955, into a strict Irish Catholic family. I was the seventh of eight children. The first seven of us were born in as many years. The first four were boys, the next two were girls, then me and my little sister.

The very first recollection I have is from when I was three years old. It was the day my parents brought my little sister Sharon home from the hospital. I stood on the couch looking out the picture window. My dad drove up in front of our house and helped Mom out of the car. She carried the new baby up the sidewalk. Mom was wearing a skirt and the baby was so thickly swaddled in a blanket that I could not even see her. They came into the house and all of us kids gathered around her. I was so excited. As the second to last child, this was the first baby I had witnessed coming into the family. All the other kids accepted it as a normal event in life. But when I looked at my new baby sister, I could not comprehend how a real person could be so tiny. I thought she was precious. I wanted to hold her but I was too little, so I just stared at her. It was that moment she arrived home and I took my first look at her that I declared myself her protector. To this day, Sharon and I still have a special and deep bond.

We didn't travel together much as a family. Though I do have vague recollections of family trips to a small cabin my dad built in the Casper Mountains, as well as a few trips to Yellowstone. The first trip I recall clearly is when my family drove to Neola, Iowa in the summer of 1960; I was four. We went to visit the family farm on which my dad was raised. That farm was like heaven to me. There were cows, pigs, chickens, dogs, and cats. There was a silo that had a small chute that poured out corn, like magic. I would pull the handle on the door to the chute over and over again just to watch the kernels flow down. There were lawn snakes to catch by day and mesmerizing lightning bugs at night. One day during that vacation, we all went over to my cousin's much larger farm. There was a huge rooster with colorful feathers, a big red comb, and sharp fighting spurs on his legs. He chased me around between the barns. I was scared and ran from him. But then my oldest brother Jim rescued me and hoisted me up on his shoulders. I felt safe up there. The big rooster chasing us became a grand game as Jim darted in between the buildings with the rooster hot on his heels, flapping wings and making angry clucking sounds. The kids were running in zigzag patterns to keep away from the rooster, and laughing. I was sure life couldn't get any better than this. I loved being with my family. I felt secure with my brothers and sisters. Much of the nurturing I received growing up was from my two oldest brothers, Jim and Paul.

We had certain family traditions that became the glue holding us together through thick and thin. They established the rhythm of life. No matter what other hardships we faced, we could always count on these specific ways of moving through the calendar year.

On Sunday mornings we attended Mass, never missing a Sunday or Holy Day of Obligation. After Mass, my dad would cook breakfast, which consisted of two eggs over easy, two strips of bacon, two pieces of toast, potatoes, and a small glass of orange juice. There was a period of time when Sunday nights were special too. Mom and Dad would make three or four homemade thin-crust pizzas on our rectangular cookie sheets and we would all gather in the living room to watch *The Wonderful World of Disney*. Mom would make two large bowls of popcorn flavored with butter and salt. Being together as a family in these moments brought me so much comfort and happiness.

My mom made seven loaves of bread twice a week. Occasionally, she would also make cinnamon rolls; they were delicious. One of the highlights of the week for me was having two pieces of fresh bread hot out of the oven. That bread seemed to make everything else alright.

Many of my favorite memories from childhood revolve around birthdays and other holidays. My birthday was the one day a year when I was *the* special child. I got to choose what we'd have for dinner. My mom made an angel food cake with powdered sugar frosting to be eaten with vanilla ice cream, after the family sang "Happy Birthday" to me. I would receive one present from Mom and Dad, and a second present from my siblings who had all pooled their money for my gift. We never had other children over for a typical "birthday party"; it was always a family-only affair.

Thanksgiving was a very traditional celebration for my family, with turkey and all the typical side dishes, finished with pumpkin and pecan pies. It was delicious and I loved spending the entire day with my family. We would play touch football outside as we waited for Mom to prepare the feast.

Easter season was an important time for us too. It started with Lent, which began on Ash Wednesday. Our family was very strict with fasting and abstinence during this time. Though we never ate meat on Fridays throughout the year, it was stricter during Lent. Every Friday during Lent, we were limited to one regular meal and two snacks. Even if we were hungry, we were not allowed to eat in between these meatless meals. We were always expected to give up one special treat during the forty days, too. Even as a young boy, I gave up things like candy; but this was not a huge sacrifice since we never had many extras (like candy, soda, or store-bought cookies) hanging around the house anyway. (Though my mom frequently made cookies and desserts from scratch.) On Easter Sunday morning, we all dressed in our very best clothes and went to High Mass. The service seemed to last forever and felt like an endurance test. But after Mass we would go home to a very decadent breakfast replete with our first meat in weeks: bacon. Midday on Easter we would have a giant traditional Easter dinner of ham, candied sweet potatoes, and mashed potatoes. This was followed by "Grandma's Dessert," a special family recipe similar to a cheesecake. This was our first taste of anything sweet in about six weeks (a lifetime for a young child), and we were absolutely thrilled. We always dyed Easter eggs, too, but Easter Sunday itself was more of a holy day and a breaking of the Lenten fast.

As memorable as these holidays were, Christmas was my favorite time of year. It wasn't only the presents that I loved, it was the season itself. For us, the season started four weeks before Christmas with the placing of an Advent wreath on the center of our kitchen table. This wreath had four candles, one representing each week of the season. Three of the candles were white, and the fourth was purple. Every night before dinner, my dad would read the Advent prayer for that day, and light a candle. The second week, two candles would be lit, and so forth. By the fourth week, all four candles would be lit at the start of dinner and remain aflame until dinnertime was over. When all of the candles were lit, we knew we were ever closer to the big day. Sometime in the middle of Advent, we would go as a family up into the mountains to select and cut our own Christmas tree. When we got it home, we would begin putting up the modest decorations that characterized the season for us. We never had snow globes or the miniature, light-up Christmas villages in our own house, but I had seen them in stores and other people's homes and thought they were absolutely magical. Christmas Eve was the start of the biggest part of our celebration. Our family would exchange gifts; the siblings drew one name and that sister or brother would be the person to whom they'd give a present. Each child also gave a gift to Mom and Dad, and our parents would give each of us children a single gift. We would go to midnight Mass. Then early on Christmas morning, we would all sneak down to the Christmas tree. There would be eight stockings (handsewn by Mom) hung on the fireplace mantel, filled with a tangerine, new toothbrush, small tube of toothpaste, Life Savers, and a small toy. Then, each of us received one big (fifteen-dollar) present from Santa.

In the summer of my eighth year, we moved to Grand Junction, Colorado. We had a few acres in an area west of town called the Redlands, which at that time was sparsely populated. It was a great place with miles of open land to explore. We would ride bikes and horses, inner tube down the irrigation canals, and hike in the mountains and on the desert. I loved being outside all day, coming home only for meals. One of my favorite experiences was when we went to the county dump, which was located way out in the country nestled in a small rocky ravine west of us. Dad would have me sit next to him in the cab of our old tan Chevy pickup truck and let me steer down the narrow gravel roads to the dump. What a thrill it was to drive; it made me feel so grown-up and important. When I would get home, I would tell my mom how I drove all by myself.

During my early years, Mom was continually busy with domestic chores. She would buy reams of fabric for our parochial school uniforms and spend the month before school making them for us. I would sit and watch her and occasionally she would let me cut some material or thread. She would buy bushels of peaches, apricots, beans, and any other produce she could get as seconds from the farmers and she would make (and can) jam for us to eat throughout the year. My mom seemed to be doing something all the time, so any affection she gave me seemed extra special—like precious nuggets of gold. When my oldest brother left for college, my mom took a full-time job as a dietitian at the state hospital; somehow, she still did all of these chores at home even after she was employed.

Some of my good memories about my upbringing are from my teen years. Throughout high school, my parents were very supportive of my sports involvement. They came to every one of my home football games and wrestling matches, and they traveled across the Rockies one winter when I qualified for the state wrestling tournament in Denver. When I was a junior, a veterinarian from Colorado State University—an institution with a renowned veterinary training program—came to my high school for Career Night. My dad accompanied me to this event as he knew I had wanted for a long time to become a veterinarian. There were only a few of us students who wanted to meet with the visiting veterinarian to learn about the program. When it was my turn to talk with him, I told this veterinarian that I was determined to become a veterinarian. He told me not to get my hopes up—it was hard to get in and I probably wouldn't make it. This infuriated my dad, who told the veterinarian in no uncertain terms that I was smart and would accomplish anything I set out to do in life. I was shocked and elated. I had never heard my dad stick up for me or talk about me like that. That really made me feel good and I thanked my dad.

I carried all of these happy memories as an adult. In retrospect, these are the *only* ones on which I based my image of childhood. Susan continued to question me about my perspective, and her questions haunted me. *Did I think that starting to drink at a young age was normal? Did I think my dad's manner of punishment was too strict? Did I remember times that my mom was affectionate with me?* I began to question my own recollections and would sometimes call one of my brothers to see how they remembered our childhood. Time and again, they shared precisely the same memories of a childhood often lacking in warmth and affection. It began to dawn on me that my upbringing did not match the ideal image I had carried with me. Then a flood of bad childhood memories began to surface.

My parents never had enough time to give any of us the loving, individual attention that we craved as children. I don't remember ever sitting on a parent's lap, being hugged or held. Neither of my parents ever told me a bedtime story. They never told me during my childhood that they loved me. The closest thing to physical contact we ever got from our mother was when we would hide behind her skirt trying to avoid my father's punishments. I also had a habit of rushing up to my mom and giving her a tremendous bear hug. Each time, she would simply respond by saying something about how strong I was and lightly patting me on the head or back.

My mother repeatedly told me I was fearless and strong; as a baby she would put me on the kitchen table and I'd courageously toddle off the edge, and when I was eighteen months old, I endured hernia surgery without any anesthetic. Another such incident occurred in first grade. A year after an accident chipping two of my teeth, one broken tooth died and had to be pulled. My father drove me to the nearest city and walked me into the cold, sterile lobby. I was terrified and reached out to hold my dad's hand, but he ignored my touch and stepped up his pace. Once in the dentist's chair, I received a lidocaine injection in my gums and the roof of my mouth that sent searing pain into my head. My body went rigid and tears involuntarily welled up in my eyes. I squeezed the armrests in order not to cry—an act that was forbidden in my family. After the painful procedure (pressure, grinding noises, and wrenching my head and teeth), my dad gave me a single aspirin for pain control. That one pill was the only medication I was given to alleviate the pain that persisted for weeks. My dad felt physical pain should be "worked through" and not masked with drugs. Now, as a father and a grandfather, I cannot fathom this. I would do *anything* I could to alleviate unnecessary pain and suffering for my own offspring.

Overall, my mom was a dominating influence in my early childhood. When I think about it now, I realize that there were times when her recurring behaviors had a negative and overbearing impact on me. There were the times when she would shut us out, for example. Our small house in Casper was across the street from an open field where I would go with my brother Mike to catch horned toads in the sagebrush. Mike was the fourth boy and the closest brother to me in age. On Saturday mornings he and I often arose early, and we would sneak out to play in the field. But when we would cross the street back to our own house, we often found that my mom had locked all the doors. My mom wouldn't let us back in until breakfast time; this seemed to be a punishment for playing outside without permission. We would just sit on the front steps together and wait to be let in. We were just two little, hungry boys who had gone outside to play in the early morning.

Dad also dominated us, but in a different way. There were many times I was disciplined harshly by my dad. The following incident illustrates the pattern of punishments I endured for normal childhood indiscretions.

One day my older sister and I were teasing each other, but it escalated into a physical fight: she gouged my shoulder with her fingernail, drawing blood, and I hit her back. My mom came into the room and wielded her usual tool. "Wait until your dad gets home!" I knew *exactly* what that meant. For the rest of the day, I was filled with an escalating fear. I could barely eat dinner. As bedtime drew closer, my terror heightened. I kept my Fruit of the Loom underwear on under my pajamas as if that would actually soften the blow. I crawled into the top bunk of our bedroom and my brother turned off the lights. He and I didn't chatter before bed that night, as usual. We knew what was coming.

I always slept on my back, except for the nights when I expected punishment. This saved me the step of rolling over later. The hour between when I went to bed and when Dad arrived home seemed like an eternity. I lay there in the dark waiting and listening. Finally, I heard the front door close, a signal that my father was home. I heard him walking slowly down the stairway and the hall, rhythmically snapping his belt as he approached our bedroom. He did not turn on the light or say a word. He just came over to our bunk bed. With his left hand, he pulled off my blankets, keeping the belt tight in his right hand. He began to spank me on my bottom with the belt, hard and repeatedly. For the eight or ten blows I suffered, I just lay there unmoving and silent. I had learned to pretend during the beatings that I was asleep because this made them go faster. Very early in my life, I had also learned not to cry because that made him spank me more. I would focus my attention on the victims I had heard about in school: entire races of people who had suffered catastrophic hardships. And for those few moments, my hardship felt insignificant compared to theirs.

Finally, the spanking would end. I just lay there in pain. Even after my father left the room, I did not cry. I lay there on my stomach because it hurt too much to sleep on my back. I was emotionally exhausted from the intense anxiety of waiting all day, and physically exhausted from the punishment. After a few minutes my brother would ask if I was okay and I would say, "yes." But he knew otherwise; my brothers had been through the same experience. During the numerous spankings my brothers received, I felt more anguish than during my own; I hated to witness this. I finally fell into a fitful sleep. As soon as I sat up the next morning, I was reminded of the spanking and the pain stayed with me for the entire day. At breakfast my parents did not say a word about what had transpired the night before.

I just accepted the pain as part of life, and I always thought I must deserve these spankings. Why else would my father punish me so severely unless I was a bad child doing evil things? This was the beginning of feeling like I was inherently a bad person, and I was ashamed.

The lack of comfort, support, or tenderness from my dad showed itself in other ways too. Once, when I was five or six years old, I sat with my family watching television in the living room. The show we were watching was very scary. I really had to go to the bathroom, but I did not want to go by myself. I waited as long as I could, and then went down the hallway toward the bathroom. But I was too scared to go in by myself. I went back into the living room and told my dad I was afraid and asked him to come with me. He said that there was nothing to be scared about and sent me back to the bathroom. But I stood there just waiting and wishing somebody would go with me. Finally, my father impatiently got up and took me by the hand into the bathroom. He told me to stay there until I wasn't scared anymore. Then he turned the lights off, shut the door, and went back into the living room to watch television. I stood there alone in the pitch-black bathroom trying not to cry for what seemed like an eternity. Eventually the fear gave way to a feeling of numbness. As an adult, I realize that I did not learn the lesson my father was trying to convey: to be fearless. Instead, I learned not to tell people when I was afraid and not to ask for help.

Once when I was nine, I was out having fun and lost all track of time. We always had supper at six o'clock and we were expected to be sitting at the table on time with hands and face washed. I arrived home forty-five minutes late and was greeted by my angry father. He made me walk down to the willow bush near our house and cut a fresh switch with which he would spank me. It was nerve-racking: I knew from many previous experiences that a flimsy one would increase the number of swats I would receive and a large one would leave welts on my bottom and legs. I cut a carefully selected switch and removed all the leaves from it. I walked back up the hill, received many swats, and was sent to bed without dinner.

Another way we were disciplined was having to sit on a tall stool next to Dad at the dinner table. If we had gotten into trouble that day, we had to sit on his left and be absolutely perfect during the meal. One particular evening I was placed there after getting in trouble at school for telling jokes in the back of the room. As I sat there at the dinner table, I was having a hard time sitting still; the next thing I knew my father backhanded me across the face. I went flying off the stool, into the wall, and the stool fell on top of me. I meekly stood up, righted the stool, and sat there totally quiet for the rest of the meal.

When I was eleven, we moved to a farm on Orchard Mesa. I was getting in trouble less frequently for my antics, but I still clowned around too much at school. Dad had given the assistant principal permission to use his paddleboard on me if he felt I needed it. During my seventh- and eighth-grade years, I made frequent trips to the assistant principal's office. One incident that ended up with a spanking was when I was caught with a small mirror I was using to reflect sunlight onto the back of the teacher's head during class and everyone was laughing. The teacher turned around but I was not quick enough. The light reflected right into her eyes. This offense brought me five swats with a wooden paddle. These spankings were repeated and doubled by my father at home later that day.

The summer after eighth grade, I came home on a really hot day from a farm job. I went to the basement where I had my leathercraft shop and where I put together model cars and airplanes. I really enjoyed building models and had been doing so since I was eight. But when I went into the room, all of my models, paints, and glue were gone. I thought that maybe one of my brothers had borrowed them. I went up to the second floor where my brother and I slept, and *all* of my toys had been cleared out of our room. The Matchbox vehicles I had been collecting for years, with my favorites lined up on the windowsill, were nowhere to be found. Some had been extra special gifts from my maternal Grandpa Herder, who had always been very kind to me and my siblings. An electric race car set my brother and I had received as our joint present for Christmas four years earlier—but which we still played with—was gone. The comic book collection that my brother and I had purchased ourselves over the years (and that stood four feet tall in the corner of our bedroom) was gone. My BB gun, all of my other toy guns, and every toy I had ever possessed were all gone. I panicked. How could this be?

I went downstairs and asked my father if he knew where all of my toys were. He looked at me and calmly said that he had given them all to a poor family that "really needed them." He wouldn't tell me where he had taken them. I did not have the nerve to confront my father to tell him that I had worked hard to earn the money to buy the toys that hadn't been gifts, that I still loved and played with them, and that *our* family was really poor. He just took every toy I owned while I was at my after-school job. Everything. There was no vestige left of my childhood. That day, things changed. I wasn't spanked anymore. It was as if my childhood were over. From that day onward, I seemed to be on my own as far as decision-making went. Apparently, that part of my parents' job was done.

Our family often faced difficult economic times. Many of my clothes were hand-me-downs from my older brothers. All of us had patches on our jeans, and we only got one new pair a year. We even had patches on some of our patches, especially on the knees. The worst, though, was when we had patches in the crotches of our jeans. It was both uncomfortable and embarrassing. I recall one eighteen-month period during which our diet consisted of cereal in the morning, one small sandwich for lunch, and rice and beans for dinner. Every day we ate the same three meals. Sometimes I put ketchup on the beans to make them more palatable.

I observed my older brothers working and having money of their own. Sometimes they would bring home goodies after work: doughnuts, Kentucky Fried Chicken, flavored cereal. I saw from my brothers that if a child earned his own money, he could buy little extravagances and treats. So, from the time I was very young, I found paid work. In fact, I began as a little entrepreneur with a chicken business that I started at the age of nine. I began raising Rhode Island Red chickens and selling any extra eggs our family didn't use for twenty-five cents a dozen. With eight children to feed there were not many extra eggs, but I sold what I could. I eventually bought, sold, and slaughtered chickens in addition to selling the eggs. By the time I was eleven, I was farming and raising livestock (pigs, steer, and a horse I owned and helped train). I began working for Burt, a farmer who lived about five miles away. Burt happened to rent and farm the forty-acre alfalfa field across from where I lived. I would walk three miles from junior high school to Burt's farm, and work until dark. He would drive me home. Essentially, he mentored me in all things farming and livestock.

Then in the summer before my final year of junior high school, I took over from Burt the renting and farming of that alfalfa field. I was responsible for fertilizing, irrigating, cutting, baling, selling, and hauling the harvest to customers. Burt would provide the equipment and fertilizer while I did the rest. We split our profits fifty-fifty. But because I was still too young to drive when I started this work, I had to hire another kid who already had his driver's license to drive the flatbed truck with the alfalfa bales to our customers. The next year, I branched out and began renting corn fields on neighboring farms, in addition to the cornfield I worked by myself that was on my dad's farm. Burt would still provide equipment, fertilizer, and the corn seed; we continued to split the profits. I also worked for a neighbor on his potato farm when it wasn't the growing season on my rented properties.

I spent the rest of my youth irrigating fields, learning to grow crops, and attending auctions to buy and sell pigs. I learned how to earn my own money, invest and reinvest in livestock, and care for animals. I modeled my behavior after the ranchers I met: weathered "Marlboro men" who showed little emotion. At auctions, I observed the vets checking the livestock and was amazed by their ability to determine the cause and cure of various diseases. I sought them out and asked questions about their lives as veterinarians. It wasn't long before I knew that this was the life I wanted to lead as a grown-up. The seed for deciding to become a vet had been sown. I had been told it was difficult to get accepted into veterinary college and I would need to dedicate myself to my studies. So, this is what I did.

While very responsible and hardworking as a child and youth, I also began to nurture my wilder side. I liked to play, take risks, experiment, and to push the limits of acceptable behavior. It was during this stage of my life that I was first introduced to alcohol. My parents never drank in front of us. But I had a friend who would sneak alcohol from his parents' liquor cabinet. When I was thirteen, he invited me and another friend to the small trailer in which he lived; his mom and dad were alcoholics and lived in another trailer next door to his. When we arrived, he produced a full fifth of Jim Beam. With little hesitation, I took the bottle and downed my first swig of straight whiskey. My eyes and throat burned at first, and then a warm, soothing feeling came over me. I was hooked. Between the three of us, we finished off the bottle and spent the evening roaming the countryside, swimming in irrigation ditches, running across the freeway, and breaking into an abandoned warehouse. When we returned to the small trailer in the middle of the night, we were covered in mud from head to foot. We hosed off the big chunks of mud and washed our clothes in his parent's trailer. The next morning, I had a throbbing headache and nausea. In spite of how sick I felt, I knew I wanted to drink again.

There were many difficult things I continued to discover about my childhood as I persevered in therapy. As I reflect on my childhood now—more than three years into my therapy with Susan and three years deepening my life insights as I wrote this book—I have come to realize that my upbringing was not an idyllic episode of some television show. Rather, it was a combination of harsh times that were interspersed with very loving times. I understand that my parents did love me as much as they could. They carried the pain of their youth into their roles as parents. I will always love them and am grateful for all they gave me. I have also found forgiveness in my heart for them.

2

CRAFTSMANSHIP

An important aspect of who I have become emerged when I was just a young child. I discovered and nourished a creative inclination that came naturally to me. When I first started working with my hands, I felt a deep satisfaction that derived from both the process as well as the end product. The act of making things was a solitary endeavor for me, one that allowed me to think and process life as well as to actually create something tangible. I sought out this time in solitude, even in my earliest years. Throughout my life, I have continued to hone my skills and I find deep contentment in making beautiful, handcrafted items for friends, family, and myself. Though I began by buying kits and rudimentary tools, my natural aptitude for making things led me to quickly branch out into original patterns. Working creatively with my hands to fashion a unique gift that brings joy to others continues to be a driving passion of mine. The two primary mediums I work with are leather and wood.

LEATHERCRAFT

I still have to this day a seemingly insignificant piece of leather, a tiny equilateral triangle so small that most leather craftsmen would scrap it. It measures two and a half inches per side, and is cut out of a thick piece of carving leather. A leather craftsman came to our classroom at St. Joseph's School when I was ten years old. He gave each student a triangle onto which to carve our initials. The man spent an hour a week over three consecutive weeks teaching us how to carve leather. During these few sessions I learned how to draw a pattern, trace it onto leather, and carve and stamp my initial onto the leather triangle. We were taught how to finish the edge with leather lacing. This was my very first creative project. I loved the sensory aspects of making this small token; the smell of the leather and the feel of it between my fingers was very gratifying. Making this keychain brought me a sense of accomplishment. I had created something tangible and valuable. It made me feel special that I could do something no one else in my family knew how to do.

We were all given Tandy leathercraft catalogs during those lessons in leather and I took mine home, perusing it with vigor. I saw a basic leathercraft set listed for about thirteen dollars. We had also been given a certificate for a dollar off anything in the catalog. I realized that I could have my very own tools; I could be a leather craftsman. But I didn't have the money. I decided to ask my dad for the money to buy the set. I was nervous approaching him. He was sitting in his chair in the living room watching television. This was a large sum of money for him to just give to me. I showed Dad what I had made over the past few weeks at school—the leather triangle with my initial on it—and I showed him the picture of the carving set that I had eyed in the Tandy catalog. I told him how much I enjoyed leatherwork. I suspect I even made one of those childhood promises like, "I'll be better in school" or "I'll clean my room." Whatever I said, it persuaded him and, much to my surprise, he agreed to buy the set for me. Perhaps he could sense how important it was for me.

I was so happy I could barely sleep that night thinking about my leathercraft set. The next day my father drove me the five miles to the Tandy Leather Store on the east end of the main street in Grand Junction. It was a small store, but for me it contained the treasures of the world. That was my first of many purchases at that store. I met the owner, Randy, and through the years we became friends as he helped me improve my craft. I could scarcely wait to get home and open my new wonder: my key to creating masterpieces on leather. It was a great starting kit that contained a swivel knife, six stamping embossing tools, a rawhide mallet, a sponge, and four projects with carving patterns. I immersed myself in these projects and methodically finished the wallet, coin purse, key fob, and two coasters that came in the kit.

I saved the money I earned from my livestock and farming work to buy precut leather project kits as well as leather from the scrap bin. I started designing my own projects with the scraps. As my projects became more advanced, I needed more tools. I would study the Tandy catalog, circling the stamping tools I wanted. Each tool cost a bit over a dollar, but were ten percent off if I bought three or more. Each time I had saved about four dollars, I would ride my bike to the Tandy store. I learned how to make custom belts, billfolds, and purses that I sold to friends and acquaintances. I enrolled in the Al Stohlman Home Study Course. I studied how experts honed their technique. I practiced carving intricate patterns. And I purchased more sophisticated tools so I could carve tiny details into the leather. I did not just want to carve leather; I wanted to be the best leather craftsman I could be. I dreamed of being an expert. I would get lost in my work, spending hours at a time immersed in my projects. I learned to express myself through leather in a family where feelings went unexpressed.

I joined 4-H and entered many of my projects in the Mesa County Fair. I placed well and began to win purple ribbons along with a small cash prize and a gift certificate. I would buy more tools with my winnings. I developed a love of tools, feeling that they were an extension of my hands and soul as well as implements for my leather creations. When I was fifteen, I made a very complicated project: a clock with a scale replica of a western horse saddle and saddle stand. I carved detailed patterns into the leather of the saddle, the stand, and the leather background of the clock. I mounted all of it onto a handmade wooden base. I felt very proud of what I had created. I entered it in the Mesa County 4-H Fair and won "Grand Champion" in the leathercraft category. This win meant that my saddle/clock was going to the Colorado State Fair in

Pueblo. I had previously qualified several 4-H projects for the State Fair in electricity, forestry, and leathercraft, but I had never submitted one as the Grand Champion of our County Fair. I was very excited. I could not afford to go the two hundred and forty miles across the mountains to the State Fair, so I had to wait a full week for the results of the judging. Finally, my 4-H leader called. I had won "Grand Champion" at the State Fair too; I was ecstatic. I was the best leathercraft carver in the state of Colorado for 1972 with a project I had designed and created on my own.

Winning the State Fair fueled my desire to create more original projects. Then a friend commissioned me to make a saddle clock for her father. I carved a miniature saddle similar to the one I had entered into the fair. But then I customized it for her dad, including a scale replica of their ranch that I incorporated into the design. There was a lot of detail carved into this piece, including a windmill whose rotating blades told time. I also made a hummingbird clock for my mother. I drew the bird image, carved out its shape, and then dyed it with bright colors to match a hummingbird's plumage. My mom loved to watch hummingbirds buzz around our flower gardens and the feeders we had outside; this Mother's Day gift from 1973 hung in her kitchen until the day she died. Clocks became a favorite project because I favored their blend of function and beauty. As I created the clocks, I could combine my burgeoning interest in woodwork with my already-developed leather carving skills.

I started sewing leather on an antique Singer treadle sewing machine we had at home, after watching how my mom used it. I learned to make leather clothing, including vests, jackets, and chaps—staples in the cowboy world in which I grew up. I set up a small work area in the single wide trailer I lived in while going through veterinary school. I would retreat into my leather workspace and carve for an hour or two in search of much-needed respite from the pressures of studies and clinics. I truly found my solace in this small work area. But over time, my leatherworking tapered off as I finished graduate studies and began my career and family life. I did find occasional moments to carve surprises for my children, including images of their favorite storybook characters into leather. Sadly, I later lost many of my tools and supplies. I haven't carved nor worked in leather since then. My children and grandchildren still see in my house a large carved leather picture of two stallions and a six-sided leather lamp. I made both of these while I was in college. My children often ask when I will start carving leather again and if I will teach them. I feel the time is coming for me to sit down and reengage with that part of me that found so much joy and peace in leathercrafting.

WOODWORKING

I started working with wood when I was ten years old, just a year after I was introduced to leathercraft. One hot summer day, my dad was building a storage area, using his Craftsman table saw. He gave me a wood scrap and told me how to make a race car out of it. I spent the rest of that day whittling the two-square-inch shape into a soapbox derby car. I painted it blue with a white stripe down the middle to make it look sporty. I found a pair of wheels off an old Tonka toy and voilà, I had a functional custom toy. That was the beginning of something that has continued to this day. I made wooden boats to float in irrigation ditches, whittled scrap wood into animals, and fashioned bows and arrows for child's play. Because I always carried a pocket knife, I would keep an eye out for interesting pieces of wood to carve into various creations that lay within the wood's unique shape. I spent hours, days, and weeks out in the hills with a pile of wood shavings underfoot.

My formal training in basic woodworking skills and safety started in seventh-grade shop class at Orchard Mesa Junior High School. It was like walking into another world as I entered the shop room. Six large square workbenches with four workstations at each bench dominated the center of the large room. Placed strategically around the sides of the room were the power tools that we were only allowed to use under direct supervision by our shop teacher, and we each had just fifteen minutes twice a week to do so. The rest of our time was spent working with hand tools. Everyone made the same project at first: a pair of bookends with a horse head on each of them. We did get to choose the type of wood we would use for the bookends. I chose black walnut for mine. Though it is a harder wood to work with, I preferred its color and interesting grain pattern over the other wood choices.

I signed up for shop again in the eighth grade and this time spent the year making a lamp out of black walnut with a Philippine mahogany decorative animal silhouette. This project involved both woodworking and electrical wiring of the lamp. As an eighth-grader, I thought it was cool to make the lamp and then have the light come on when I pulled the chain. I was intrigued by the wide range of possibilities that learning a craft such as woodworking opened up—both decorative and functional pieces could be produced. Though I loved woodworking, I did not sign up for shop class from ninth grade on because I already knew I wanted to become a veterinarian and felt it best to concentrate on the core academic classes (sciences and math) that would help me achieve this goal. I did continue working with wood in my spare time though, incorporating it into my leather projects.

But in the summer after my freshman year of undergraduate studies, I started my true apprenticeship in woodworking. I began working with an accomplished carpenter and cabinetmaker, Jim Whaley, learning how to frame custom houses, do remodels, and build cabinets. I spent the next six summers working for him. At first, I learned how to make rough cuts and do projects that didn't require extreme accuracy. But as my skills grew, I became involved with more of the cabinetmaking work which requires exacting measurements and perfect attention to (and execution of) detail. I loved it when my pieces fit perfectly. During those years, my obsession with woodworking tools started. My brother Paul and I would retreat into his workshop over my Christmas breaks and make presents for our family.

I graduated from Colorado State Veterinary College in May 1980 when I was twenty-four years old. I moved to Cottage Grove, Oregon, for my first job. I was given an office in the clinic but there was no desk. I spent my evenings that first month making my own desk. With the limited budget of a new graduate, I purchased one sheet each of three-quarter-inch, half-inch, and quarter-inch plywood and some one-inch dimension lumber. I built a standard-size seven-drawer desk with only my hand tools. I have this desk in my upstairs office to this day.

Through the years, I have used my woodworking skills in a wide range of projects. I have completed large-scale projects such as designing and building kitchens, constructing and remodeling houses, doing subsequent clinic remodels, and building a three-thousand-square-foot workshop. I have also designed and made countless small and intricate projects such as jewelry boxes, pens, Christmas and holiday ornaments, toys, shadow boxes, jungle gyms, and a scale-model kitchen for my little girls to play in, as well as assorted small (and personalized) gifts for my children and grandchildren. My grandchildren now play with many of the wooden toys I once made for my children. As "Pops" (father and grandfather), I also create wooden templates (often with holiday themes) that the youngest family members can then decorate to their liking.

At any given time, I probably have more than a dozen woodworking projects in production as well as several designs in process for future projects. It seems as if I never run out of ideas for home or clinic improvements, gifts for others, or upgrades to older woodworking projects. Currently—and as a "fun" side project—I am helping design a new state-of-the-art emergency veterinary clinic for our region. My craftsman skills seem to be endlessly useful. To see my ideas take shape—through time, effort, and process—as tangible and aesthetically pleasing objects is a continual source of pleasure and fulfillment. I cannot envision my life without a workshop and creative endeavors to indulge. I am deeply passionate about my work as a veterinarian and know that it was what I was called to do. I also know that had I not been chosen for that fulfilling and rewarding career, I might well have found myself working as an artistic craftsman, creating custom-designed functional pieces that in-corporate wood, leather, and perhaps other materials.

3

FIRST LOVES

The summer of 1971 for me was the summer of travel, adventure, and my first love. I was fifteen years old. I had been selected as one of forty outstanding 4-H youth members from the Western Slope of Colorado to travel by charter bus for three weeks on an exchange trip to Austin, Texas. Once I knew I was going on the trip, I had to secure help with my farm while I was away; I would be gone in the middle of the prime growing and harvesting season. I worked long days in early June so all the cornfields were cultivated and irrigated before I left. I mowed and baled the forty acres of alfalfa and hired five of my high school friends to help me put up the first cutting of hay. I hired one of these friends to irrigate the corn and the alfalfa while I was gone. The second cutting of alfalfa could wait until I returned. I was both excited and nervous to go. I had never been separated from my family for weeks at a stretch, nor had I ever traveled that far away from home. I only knew six or eight of the other exchange students and only one of the adults who would be traveling with us.

The 4-H members and six adult chaperones met in downtown Grand Junction on the mid-June morning we were starting the trip. I noticed Susie that first day. She was the prettiest girl on the bus. She was five-feet four-inches with light blonde hair that came down below her shoulders. On the second day, I worked up the nerve to introduce myself. She was easy to talk with. She had the nicest smile and gentlest laugh. I started sitting in seats close to Susie, and I made a point to greet her every morning and talk with her when the bus made a stop. At our first major excursion, the National Cowboy and Western Heritage Museum in Oklahoma City, I was one of the last to get on the bus. I liked to stay in the fresh air as long as possible before spending those long hours on the bus. One of the only vacant seats was next to Susie. She usually sat with one of her girlfriends, but this time she was alone. I asked her if I could sit down with her. She smiled and said "yes," and so down I sat. I was a little shy at first, but soon we were laughing and talking. From then on, I tried to sit with her whenever I could.

Susie was my first girlfriend and I liked the nervous, happy feeling I had when I was around her. Being with her was so easy and it added a level of excitement to the trip I had never imagined. She was two years older than I was and a grade ahead of me in school. She had recently broken up with her first boyfriend. He had not been nice to her. I couldn't understand how anybody could be mean to someone as sweet as Susie. She and I became inseparable during the trip: sitting next to each other on the bus, eating in the restaurants, and walking around outside on breaks or when we were viewing various attractions.

Somewhere between Shreveport and New Orleans, I fell in love with Susie. It was my first love: a young love, a puppy love. But for me it was real love. I had never felt these emotions before. I was excited in the mornings at the thought of seeing Susie, nervous that I would say something stupid and she would quit sitting by me, and hopeful that she liked me half as much as I liked her. I loved feeling in love. To have someone for whom I cared so much return that attention made me feel special. I was sure no one else had ever felt such an intense love before. I was all in. By the time the bus rolled in to New Orleans, Susie and I had become an official couple. We sat together as we drove through the French Quarter and through the large antebellum mansions lining the roads in the Garden District. We held hands as we went on a guided walking tour of the aboveground tombs in the cemetery area of New Orleans. We shared our dual excitement of being together and seeing a place that seemed exotic to us.

From New Orleans, we traveled to Galveston where we had a feast of fresh caught seafood. It was on the sandy beaches of Galveston, Texas, overlooking the Gulf of Mexico that we had our first kiss. It was awkward, it was clumsy, and it was sublime. It was an innocent kiss. We could have stayed on that beach in each other's arms forever.

Our next stop was Austin, where we stayed for five days with separate families that had 4-H members about our age. From Austin, we drove across Texas into New Mexico to the Carlsbad Caverns. We drove across New Mexico and stopped in Santa Fe in time to catch an evening rodeo.

Toward the end of the trip, Susie and I were sad as we contemplated leaving each other. The last three weeks had been special for both of us. We only lived forty miles apart, but it might as well have been four hundred miles. I would not have my driver's license for another month and a half, and her dad would not let her drive down to Grand Junction alone. We exchanged phone numbers and addresses. The day the bus pulled back into that same parking lot we had been in three weeks prior, Susie and I were on the verge of tears. I held her hand as we left the bus and I gave her a little hug. But I could not kiss her goodbye in front of our parents.

Susie and I stayed true to our promises to each other and kept in touch. I would write her letters twice a week and she would write back. In almost every letter I sent, I would write a four-line poem in the upper right corner. The poem would be about us, nature, or my feelings. I would often include a pressed flower or small trinket inside the envelope. We called each other once or twice a week, but because long-distance calls were expensive we could not talk long. It was hard for us to be away from each other.

The first time we saw each other after our trip was when Susie came down to Grand Junction a month later to participate in a 4-H sewing competition in early August. It was held in the high school auditorium in the middle of town. I sat in the auditorium next to her older sister and her mother. Susie modeled a maroon full-length gown she had designed and sewn. Her hair was styled. I could not believe how gorgeous she looked. When I saw her up on stage, I felt my love for her grow even stronger. I was so proud to have her as my girlfriend. The afternoon ended all too quickly and she had to go back home.

In late August, my sixteenth birthday arrived: the long-awaited day on which I would get my driver's license. I had football practice that morning and my dad took me down to the license bureau at noon. I took my driver's test and passed. I had football practice again that afternoon and I drove myself. After practice I came home, showered, and changed into nice clothes. I got into the Plymouth Satellite I had purchased for eight hundred dollars from my older brother and I drove the forty miles up the mountain canyon to Susie's house. I was nervous. I had never driven this far alone. It was great to see Susie and to celebrate my birthday with her.

Throughout my junior year, I drove up to see Susie almost every weekend, even during the snowy Colorado winter. I would pick her up, drive back to Grand Junction, take her to dinner and a movie, and then drive her back home. It was a journey of a hundred and sixty miles, and worth every mile of it to be with Susie. I came to know the Plateau Valley Canyon curves quite well. The summer after my junior year, I worked on a ranch owned by Red, my high school math teacher. His ranch was up in Collbran, close to Susie's home. I had my own small bunkhouse and I worked long, hard days. Susie and I spent some evenings and the bulk of Saturday evening and Sundays together that summer. We spent our time going to movies, riding horses, having picnics in the mountains, or going for rides on my motorcycle. And we talked a lot; there was always easy conversation between us. That was one of the happiest summers of my life.

The following school year and summer, the geographic distance between us precluded Susie and I from spending so much time together; Susie was hours away in college, and I was busy farming and studying hard in high school. But we continued to enjoy our time together on the sporadic weekends we had, and our relationship remained strong.

The fall of 1973, I entered Colorado State University to start my studies and Susie went back to Western State College. Now we were a five-hour drive away from each other. I made the trip twice the first quarter and she visited me once. Our relationship was now being strained by the distance between us. I came home for Thanksgiving that year and found a letter from Susie waiting for me there. It was my first "Dear John" letter. She said it was too hard to only see me sporadically and that she had found someone else. I was crushed. My first romantic love lasted three and a half years and ended because of the geographic distance between us.

After that, I was not in a serious relationship for about a year. I was a student assistant at a coed dorm and met Brenda, a freshman from Illinois. We started dating and our relationship lasted two years. We loved and cared for each other. But we drifted apart during my first semester of veterinary school. She wanted a firm commitment and marriage. I loved Brenda, but I could not see myself getting married while I was in vet school. I was very sad, but I did understand this breakup.

Then I met Jan, a forestry major in her sophomore year. Jan and I seemed to be made for each other. She loved the outdoors and we would go hiking in the mountains to get away from the pressures of school. Her best friend dated a player on my rugby team. Jan enjoyed the rugby crowd and attended every game she could. We went skiing together. She was smart, witty, and driven. She enjoyed dancing to country music. And she always kept me in line if I was acting up. On top of all that, she was a person I could talk to about anything. She understood me and my inner demons. She was strong in ways I was not. I fell in love with Jan, and the more time we spent together, the stronger my love grew. I loved her with all my heart, and we talked about marriage when I graduated. I took her home and my family liked her. Jan and I were inseparable for my first three years of veterinary school. Everything was going well between us.

Then I suddenly lost my best friend, Vern. I started drinking more to cope with my pain. Jan tried to help but I was lost and angry at the world. I closed down emotionally and shut her out just when I needed her the most. She had just graduated and was working across the mountains for the U.S. Forest Service. We would see each other occasionally. But I realize now that my drinking and utter emotional chaos drove her away from me. Our love remained, but it was not enough to overcome my depression. Instead of letting her love support me through my first major life tragedy, I chose to turn to alcohol.

I lost my best friend and my true love that same year.

4

VERN AND DAVE

I met Vern at the beginning of my freshman year of undergraduate studies at Colorado State University. We had some friends in common and we would all drink together. But within a few weeks, Vern and I had developed a deep bond. He was from my hometown and his ranch was only five miles from my family's farm. We quickly became very close friends, like kindred spirits. Though we had met in bars while drinking, Vern and I also had in common a commitment to study very hard. He was conversant in a lot of subjects and was quite intelligent.

It wasn't just our upbringing that bound us. Vern and I both found deep contentment in caring for the land and the livestock about which we were passionate. We came from agriculture backgrounds and could easily talk about raising cattle, calving experiences, irrigating, crops, and the process of farming land. Vern and I had both learned and deeply valued the importance of working hard. We took many animal science classes together and we did very well because we already had the practical knowledge of farming and ranching. We also shared the core values of honesty, kindness, and empathy for others. Family came first for us; we had strong connections to our own families of origin. And both of us envisioned a future being married to a loving wife and raising children in the countryside.

During the seven years I knew Vern, we had a diverse range of shared experiences. Every year at the huge, weeks-long National Western Stock Show in Denver, I would go down on weekends to help Vern show his Hereford bulls. We took day trips together, went on double dates, and hung out with our group of friends. One or two weekends a month, we would head up to the mountains to hike the slopes of the Rockies. We enjoyed country western concerts. In short, we excelled in school and took the pressure off by having fun.

Vern made the hard work of my college days easier with his sense of humor and his friendship. We had become inseparable throughout our college years. Vern and I were like brothers. After four years, he graduated with his B.S. in Animal Science and went back to work at his family's ranch in Whitewater, near my childhood home. He was going to take over the running of the ranch.

Every time I went home to visit my family, I would also visit Vern and his new wife, Connie Jo. They had met in college, fallen deeply in love, and gotten married the summer before our senior year. As a groomsman at their wedding, I saw how deeply bonded and happy they were together. I grew closer to them even after Vern had graduated and began married life. Whenever I made the eight-hour drive across the Rocky Mountains from school to home, I would be sure to spend time with Vern and Connie Jo on their ranch. Occasionally we would go out to drink, but mostly we'd work together; I'd help him with his livestock and other ranch projects. Vern and I were easy collaborators with our shared passions, knowledge, and extensive practical experience.

On Memorial Day weekend 1979—my senior year of veterinary college—I went home to see my family and friends, as usual. That Monday I stopped to have lunch at the ranch with Vern, Connie Jo, and their six-month-old daughter Andi. I couldn't believe how big their baby had gotten since my last visit. Vern beamed and exuded pride as a new father, and I felt how much he loved his baby girl. Likewise, Connie Jo radiated joy in her role as a new mother. Connie Jo handed Andi to me and I, too, immediately felt the magic of their little baby girl. I loved holding her. It brought me so much peace to cradle this tiny being in my arms. Connie Jo fixed us a nice lunch and we talked for a couple of hours. Finally, I had to leave as I was starting summer quarter and had clinics the next day. At midday, I left Vern's and drove back across the mountains to school.

Early the next morning, I was awakened by the ringing of my phone. My dad told me that Vern had died the day before. I thought he must be telling a terrible joke. It was inconceivable to me. I had just seen Vern less than twenty-four hours before and he was happy and healthy. Dad explained how, shortly after I had left, Vern went out to irrigate his hay pasture. He was struck by lightning and killed instantly. When he did not return from the fields, Connie Jo went out and found him lying in the pasture, dead. I was in shock as I heard this news. I hung up the phone and cried. Once I composed myself, I went into school and told them what had happened, and that I needed to return home that day. I was numb as I drove back across the Rockies. They were the same roads I had driven the day before, but I was a different person. I had never felt such pain. I drove straight to Connie Jo's and we held each other, crying. I told her I would do anything to help her. She asked me to give Vern's eulogy at his service; Connie Jo told me that everyone in her and Vern's family wanted me to do this. That was the hardest speech I have ever given. I did not know how to talk about the pain of losing such a wonderful person. I talked about how loving a person Vern had been and how much he adored Connie Jo and Andi. I said that the good are often taken too early and that God must have needed a good cowboy in heaven. But no matter what I said, there was no way I could convey my love for him and the pain of my loss. His service was in Grand Junction (fifteen miles from his ranch), and the next day we all drove down to Durango for his burial in Connie Jo's hometown. I was one of six pall-bearers who carried Vern to his final resting place.

After a week with Connie Jo and Vern's family, I had to return to vet school. The grief I felt was immense. I had never before lost anyone I loved and to whom I was so close. I was absolutely and totally emotionally destroyed. I had to resume my studies. But it was extremely

difficult to be present and focused with the enormity of grief I was experiencing. During the day I did the best I could in clinics. But when I
went home at night—and I was alone—I turned to alcohol. It was the
first time I had used booze as a tool to assuage my pain. I lost control. I
remember one time when I regained consciousness in the middle of the
road after wrecking my motorcycle. People were all around me, asking
if I was okay. I just got up and rode off. I couldn't drink enough to end
the agony. So, I drank more.

I drank excessively and continually. I could barely function. I used
what little energy I had to focus on my studies and to try to succeed in
graduate school. My drinking pattern up to this point had been one of
abstinence and overindulgence. I could go weeks without drinking when
my studies, sports activities, or work required total focus. But then I'd go
on a bender; I would drink excessively on a weekend or for a whole week
at a time. In retrospect, I realize that when I picked up the first drink I
was all in. I was fostering a life that alternated between exceedingly hard
work and overachievement, and a life of using alcohol to either celebrate
or to cope. This became the pattern from age thirteen to sixty.

This is the same pattern that caused me to push away Jan and lose
that relationship.

I did make it through my senior year of graduate school, but I never
worked through my emotional pain from losing Vern. There's an emptiness in my heart I have never filled.

A year and a half after graduation, I traveled from Oregon back home
to Colorado. I visited my friends at CSU. I learned that another one of
my closest friends in vet school, Dave Adams, had died in his sleep two
months earlier from a congenital heart problem that nobody had known
about. I collapsed and cried in the corridor outside the room where a
mutual acquaintance had just shared the news of Dave's passing. I was

in total shock. Three months prior, I had spent a week in Wyoming with Dave. And now he, too, was gone.

Dave had been very athletic, playing intramural football with me. After Vern's death, Dave and I had become even closer. I had not heard from Dave in the past couple of months and wondered why. No one knew how to reach me where I was working in Oregon in order to tell me this tragic news. Dave's wife was pregnant when he died. His baby daughter was born a few months after his passing. I never had the chance to meet his new daughter or to offer my sympathies to his wife; they had moved and none of us knew how to reach her in their new residence in New York City. Here was another dear friend who had died just as his dreams were being fulfilled. I was thrown back into the dark pain I had barely come to accept from Vern's death. That night, I turned again to alcohol. I just couldn't believe it. Two of my closest friends gone in eighteen months. When I drove home to visit my parents, I found a present that Dave had sent to me a few months earlier. I sat with the gift on my lap and wept again.

My friendships with Vern and Dave were very important ones that I lost too early and forever. I wonder how Vern and I would be today as older men looking back on our youth, our careers, and our families. I imagine Dave and I would have rendezvoused at annual veterinary conferences, swapping stories about our lives and work. I suspect that these two relationships would have grown deeper with so many more life experiences that we would have shared over the years. These are things I will never know. All I can do now is carry the memories of these two dear friends in my heart as I travel through life as a middle-aged man with children and grandchildren of my own.

5

ESTABLISHING A
PROFESSIONAL PRACTICE

The first professional position I held as a veterinarian was in Cottage Grove, Oregon, in a practice that provided health care to a myriad of animals. We treated pets (mostly dogs and cats), as well as farm animals: horses, cows, goats, and pigs. I had driven from Fort Collins in my 1965 Dodge pickup truck pulling an old wooden-sided trailer that carried my blue Yamaha motorcycle along with all of my worldly possessions. I had eight hundred and fifty dollars in cash to start out my new life as a veterinarian. The practice that I was joining had me working every weekday plus every other Saturday. Two Sundays a month I also worked at the small, local livestock auction in nearby Creswell. I felt so much a part of that scene, as it reminded me of all those days I had gone to the auction back home. I met the local farmers and ranchers as I walked up and down the alleyways examining the animals' medical fitness. I would perform health exams, do pregnancy checks, and draw blood, sending home livestock with contagious conditions to ensure the health and integrity of the animals being sold at auction. People buying animals would ask me questions about the animals for sale, just like I had questioned the veterinarians at the livestock auction back in Fruita, Colorado, as a teenage entrepreneurial farmer. I so enjoyed my Sunday afternoons at the auction that it hardly seemed like work.

One of the rites of passage for me as a large-animal veterinarian was the first day I went out alone on calls to farms. After riding around with the senior veterinarian for three weeks, he felt I was ready to go out and treat animals by myself. I was excited to put my knowledge to work curing animals. I had three calls scheduled for that day. I checked the truck, making sure I had everything I would need: medicines and supplies, directions to the farms I'd be visiting, the medical records for each animal I would need to treat, and a full gas tank in the practice's medically equipped Suburban. Though eager to be on my own, I also felt a bit anxious without a seasoned vet by my side to offer advice and approve my decisions.

My first call that day was to check on a sick Hereford cow located on a ranch in a beautiful valley outside of Drain, a small ranching community eighteen miles south of Cottage Grove. I had been down there twice in the last week with the senior vet. Blood tests had shown liver disease in this cow, so we had formulated a treatment plan for her. On the way down, I considered which drugs I would need and how I might administer them (either intravenously or intramuscularly). I pulled up to the barnyard and opened the truck door.

As I was stepping out of the truck, I heard a gunshot echo up the small canyon in which the ranch was located. It totally startled me. I wondered what the rancher had done. He came into view almost immediately, with the still-smoking pistol in his right hand. "Couldn't take it. I took care of 'er." At first, I was confused about what he meant. But then I quickly realized he had shot the cow I was there to treat. She was my first patient on my first day solo as a vet, and all I could do was a postmortem exam on her because I had no idea what else to do with my dead patient. We knew the cause of death (gunshot), but we still needed to find out why the cow's liver disease had been so severe; we needed to know if the other cows in the rancher's herd were at risk. Just as I had been taught in vet school, I performed a complete necropsy to examine all of her organs; this is a very involved, physically demanding procedure. When I cut through the Hereford's liver, I found liver flukes—an internal parasite that cows get from grazing in moist pastures and ingesting snails. These liver flukes were huge, about the size of silver dollars, and they had migrated through the liver, ultimately destroying it. There was nothing we could have done to help my patient. Before I left that day, I discussed herd treatment for liver flukes with the rancher in order to curb the spread of the destruction.

My second call on my first solo day was twenty-eight miles north of where I'd spent the morning. I was to recheck a horse I had seen the previous day. It was a gelding that was lethargic and hadn't eaten in several days. I had sent in his blood for analysis but had not received the results yet. The owner had to be at work and couldn't meet me, so I told her I would take care of the horse on my own. When I arrived, the horse was nowhere in sight. I was puzzled. I walked around for about fifteen minutes. Finally, I spotted four hooves sticking up out of the drainage ditch on the far side of the pasture. I hurried over and found the horse lying dead on his back. *Damn.* I performed my second necropsy of the day and collected samples of the organs. The liver appeared fibrotic and diseased. The results from the blood tests and tissue samples later showed that the horse died of tansy ragwort poisoning, a commonly found toxic plant. I came to hate that plant as I treated an increasing number of horses and cows during my time in Oregon; often my efforts to save the livestock who had grazed on the ragwort were unsuccessful. As I left the farm that late morning, I muttered aloud to myself, "Two for two of my patients are dead. This is not good."

My third and final call of my first solo day was at a farm just a couple of miles away. It was for a three-hundred-and-fifty-pound sow the owner felt was having trouble farrowing (progressing through labor). When I looked at the pig over the fence lying in the middle of a large dusty corral, she sure didn't look like she was in labor. As a matter of fact, she didn't even look pregnant to me. When I voiced my opinion to the sow's owner, she stared at me and told me her pig definitely was pregnant and in distress. She insinuated I didn't know what I was talking about. After having both of my previous patients die, I felt she might be right. There was no area in which to confine the sow, and the woman offered no help. I decided I needed to catch and then tranquilize the sow, but at that time there were no good drugs that reliably worked to sedate a pig.

Consequently, I spent the next two hours chasing the sow around a dusty corral in ninety-degree heat. I was able to occasionally get an injection into her that I hoped would slow her down. Four injections later, the sow was still active. I went inside to call the senior vet for advice; he had none. Over time, the neighbors came to watch the debacle, but no one offered any help. I had become the spectacle for the farmers lounging on the railings of the corral observing the fruitless chase. Finally, the sow stumbled and lay down. I wasn't sure if the drugs had finally taken effect or if she was simply as exhausted as I was. I was able to touch her and to perform the briefest of reproductive exams before she arose and stumbled away. I was spent. I looked at the pig's owner and told her the sow's cervix wasn't open and that she wasn't ready to give birth.

I left that farm exhausted, dirty, and discouraged. Nothing had gone right. I hadn't saved anyone, nor did I have a shred of my pride intact. They didn't tell me about days like this when I was in vet school. I started thinking that getting back into construction might be a wise career move. I wasn't sure the animal population needed me wreaking havoc on it. *Seven years in college down the drain*, I thought. Two months later I went back to the same farm where I had the big sow chase; I was on a call to treat a goat. As much as I didn't want to bring up the subject, I nonchalantly asked the pig's owner how the sow ended up doing after that fateful day I spent chasing her. Without missing a beat, she said, "You know, she wasn't pregnant after all." It took all I had to keep quiet.

A month later, I was called out at midnight to go solo on my first major emergency to assist a cow who was having trouble calving. She was a heifer (bearing her first calf), and these are the situations in which most calving problems occur. I got in the truck and drove down to the ranch where the heifer was in distress. It was one in the morning when I pulled up to the ranch. The rain was steady, and it was an extremely dark night. I asked the rancher to show me the way to his troubled heifer. He pointed up what turned out to be a steep, eight-hundred-foot mountain. But I could not see a thing. The rancher said there was a corral and barn halfway up the slope, but it was far too slick, and roadless, to be able to drive my vet truck up to her. There were no lights, either. I had a brief moment of panic wondering how I would manage this difficult case under such challenging conditions. I tried to think of everything I would need to take with me up the hill so that I could examine the heifer and help deliver her calf. There were two ranch hands to help carry the equipment up the hill. They had two old flashlights; these would be my only sources of light by which to work.

All four of us walked up the slippery wet, grassy slope to where the heifer was lying down in the middle of the corral. To make matters worse, she was a Black Angus and I could barely see the heifer in the dim beams put out by the two feeble flashlights. I examined the heifer but was unable to reposition the calf so that it could be delivered. I determined that I would need to do a cesarean section. I had assisted with several such operations on one of my vet school rotations to a calving station in Clay Center, Nebraska. But I had never done one on my own. I could not have thought of a more difficult scenario: it was the middle of the night, totally dark, raining a steady drizzle, using poor lighting to see a black heifer. We packed up all of the equipment we had hauled up the mountain to assist the heifer in birthing, and took it all back down to the truck and gathered the necessary surgical equipment I would need to do the C-section. I had to think of everything I might possibly need to perform an emergency surgery on my own and then carry it all up the hill.

Adrenaline was surging through my body. I felt like I was on a mission to save mom and baby; yet at the same time I was terrified about undertaking such a major surgery all by myself under these circumstances. But I had no choice. I carefully thought through the procedure, step by step, trying to think of every drug and instrument I would need. I knew that once I started, I would not be able to pause to go get whatever I might have forgotten. Down at the vet truck, I organized everything I needed along with my stainless steel bucket, hot water, and scrub. I gave everyone something to carry, and up the hill we trudged again.

Once I arrived back up at the corral, I shaved the left side of the heifer with a barber's straight edge razor, gave her a local anesthetic block, and did three surgical scrubs. I wasn't sure how effective my scrubs were with the continual drizzle coming down, but I figured the rain was semi-sterile. Or, at least I hoped it was. I took the scalpel blade and made a twenty-four-inch cut through the skin and then through the underlying muscles. One of the ranch hands who was holding a flashlight kept continually taking the light off the heifer to shine it on all of the cows that had congregated around the perimeter of the corral. The other cows seemed to be interested in what one of their own was going through, and the ranch hand seemed to be more interested in what they were doing than in what I was doing. I continually had to yell at him to get the flashlight back on the heifer. I cut into the uterus and reached in to grab the legs of the calf. It required all of my strength to pull him out through the incision. He was a good-sized calf, weighing about one hundred and ten pounds. I swung him upside down by his legs to clear his nose and lungs and then tied off his umbilical cord. Once I had the calf stabilized, I turned my attention back to the heifer. I sutured up the incision and administered antibiotics. I looked at my finished work and was very relieved it was over.

The mom and baby were both standing up now, and she was licking and cleaning his entire body. He wobbled back to her udder and with the help of the ranchers started nursing. It was amazing how he instinctively knew where to go and what to do. I'm still amazed to this day when I see this happen. I felt a great rush of satisfaction and accomplishment. This is exactly what I had spent all those years training to be able to accomplish. I had just experienced my first big solo emergency call to a ranch, and both mama and calf were alive and well. That night I knew I was in the right profession.

The vet practice I worked for happened to be located across from the railroad track that ran through the small town of Cottage Grove. Late one morning, a distraught logger rushed in with his huge three-year-old black Lab, appropriately named "Bear." The owner was in a state of sheer panic as Bear had just been run over by the train and his right rear leg was severed, hanging only by a remnant of flattened skin. There was blood squirting from the stump, but Bear was wagging his tail, oblivious to his pain and impending doom if left untreated. I quickly applied pressure and clamped off the artery. I started Bear on intravenous fluids and stabilized him. Then I discussed Bear's condition with the owner and told him Bear's leg needed to be amputated above the knee. At first the owner just wanted to euthanize his dog. Bear would always sit up on his back legs to greet his human whenever he would come home. That's how he got his name Bear. The pet owner was certain Bear would be unhappy if he couldn't do this. I convinced the man to let me do the amputation and if Bear wasn't happy in two weeks, I would euthanize him and not charge for the surgery. The owner agreed. Two weeks later, Bear came running into the clinic on three legs as happy as ever begging for the treat he received on every visit. The owner was ecstatic. He said Bear started sitting up on his one remaining hind leg within a few days of surgery. It was one of the many times I've been amazed at the resiliency of our animal friends.

My time at the vet clinic in Cottage Grove was very fruitful. It was a busy practice and I had a good mentor for that first professional job after vet school. A year after I started there, in the summer of 1981, I had an opportunity to work with an equine practitioner. I was contemplating moving into work that was solely horse-oriented, so I left Oregon to take a job up near Tacoma, Washington. I only worked for the equine vet for a few months. There were facets of his practice with which I felt very uncomfortable, so I gave my notice. This left me with no job.

My dream had always been to have my own veterinary practice in a small country town. This was my chance. I moved to Arlington, Washington: rural farm country with a good population of farm animals. In October 1981, I relocated, took out a loan, and set about starting my practice. I purchased a fourteen-foot step-up cargo van and spent two months building cabinets and equipping it to function as my veterinary clinic. I could examine and treat dogs and cats as well as do surgeries in the front section of the van. In the mornings, patients would come to the farm on which I lived, and I would treat their small pets in my van. I was also equipped to drive out to the local area farms to treat large animals from the back of the van; I would make these rounds in the afternoons. In this small, specially outfitted vehicle, I officially started my own first vet practice.

My first client of my practice called me in December 1981. He had a goat on his small farm up Jim Creek Road. The goat was very lame in both front legs and had enlarged, arthritic knees. I diagnosed it with caprine arthritis encephalitis, an incurable viral disease. Sadly, it was one of those dreaded times strewn throughout my career in which I had to have the difficult conversation with the owner of an animal that the situation was dire. All I could offer was pain relief and compassion.

My business grew over the next two years and I purchased a nine-hundred-square-foot house on the north side of Arlington in the spring of 1983. Though it wasn't huge, it seemed spacious compared to working out of my van. The farm calls I made were limited to large animals that couldn't travel to my new vet clinic, or to the occasional small animal whose condition made them difficult to transport.

For the first nine years of my practice, I worked alone with occasional relief on Wednesdays. I worked six days a week seeing scheduled patients, and was on call twenty-four hours a day, seven days a week. Back then, veterinarians took their own emergency calls. And emergencies were very much a part of life as a country veterinarian. Birthing problems and trauma made up a large percentage of the emergencies for which I was called out. Emergency calls to pull calves, assist mares, and help goats took me to many farms late at night. Various types of emergencies—porcupine quills, car accidents, broken legs, bear attacks, difficult labors—often brought me into the clinic late at night as well.

One of the most memorable, and for me record-setting, cesareans was on a dog. In the middle of the night, a good client called. She raised Fila Brasileiro dogs and had a female that had been in labor for over two hours. Filas are mammoth dogs weighing upward of two hundred pounds. They were bred in Brazil to hunt jaguars and to protect people's homes. My client needed me to go to her house to help get her huge dog into her van so we could take it to the clinic. I had to carry this behemoth dog who was in active labor down a very narrow, steep stairway as was often built in the older farmhouses. The only benefit to the stairwell being so narrow was that I couldn't fall sideways. There is no benefit to it being so steep. I carried the dog outside and put her into the owner's van. Off to the clinic we went.

This owner had assisted me before on C-sections, so I didn't need to give her any instructions; we just went to work. We were accustomed to litters of eight to ten puppies with her Filas, and sometimes up to a dozen in a large litter. I had planned for this many and had towels warming up in the dryer to accommodate that number of pups. I started the surgery and I would remove one puppy from the uterus, take it out of the sac, clear the mouth and nose, and hand it to the owner who would dry and rub them to help them breathe. I handed her pup after pup after pup. At ten puppies I had her put more towels in the dryer. I kept handing her puppies and she kept asking me, "Is that the last one?" I would reply, "No." After two hours, when I finally handed her the last puppy, we confirmed our count: there were seventeen puppies. It was the largest litter either of us had ever experienced. All of the puppies and the mom did very well. It was amazing.

We were both totally exhausted but happy. I think we used every towel we had in the clinic.

My practice prospered and by 1988, I was outgrowing my small clinic. I needed to increase the building size as well as to hire more staff. These were big, scary decisions that involved risk, but I felt my business was ready for the next step. I spent several months designing a clinic that would maximize the size I was allowed to construct on my city lot as well as to be efficient in client and patient flow. I started building in the spring of 1989 and for the next six months, I worked full-time at my practice, managed the construction of the addition, and then built by hand the reception desk, benches, exam tables, and all of the cabinets in the clinic in my "spare time." I set up my woodworking shop in the garage that was part of the addition. It was a colossal undertaking, but it went smoothly. I never had to close the clinic during construction, and there was only one day during which I had to divert client and patient flow. We continued to work during those six months in the original small clinic.

The addition to the clinic was finally finished in the fall. My staff and I moved into the remodeled and greatly expanded clinic; it was over four times bigger than the old one. It was beautiful and functional. The clinic included patient care on the main floor, offices upstairs, a full basement for storage, and a garage for my farm animal truck and equipment. My clients and staff loved it. Some of the staff members who went through the remodel are still working with me today. I also felt that I was ready to hire an associate veterinarian. I now had every Wednesday off, as well as every other Saturday, and was on call only half the time. It felt like I was on vacation.

I became increasingly interested in acupuncture as a way to treat health conditions that did not respond well to Western medicine. These included certain neurologic problems as well as many chronic problems such as arthritis. So, in the fall of 1994, I took the acupuncture certification course through the International Veterinary Acupuncture Society.

I attended the course in Clearwater, Florida. Two weeks before I was to attend my first class, I was presented with Timshel, a ten-year-old golden retriever. He had severe back problems and both of his rear legs were stuck in extensor rigidity, meaning that they were stiff and he could not bend them at all. I tried the various medicines available at that time, but nothing worked. His owners were considering euthanasia. I told them I was going to the acupuncture course and I would see if there was anything I would learn that might help Timshel. To say that I was initially confused by Eastern medicine is an understatement. It is a totally different paradigm and approach to health and the treatment of disease. During the course in Florida, I talked to one of the instructors about my patient, Timshel, and she told me some acupuncture points to use and I purchased acupuncture needles.

On my way home from work my first day back after taking that initial week of training, I went out to the client's house to treat Timshel. By now, Timshel had been in extensor rigidity for three weeks. I put needles in the points my instructor had shown me and left them in for fifteen minutes. After I removed the needles, I picked up Timshel to put him back on his bed. When I set him down, his legs were immediately relaxed, and he could bend them normally. We were all shocked and happily amazed. I continued to come out and treat Timshel twice a week with acupuncture. By the second week he could stand, and by the fourth week he was walking on his own. He continued to improve and went on to live three more years as a happy, mobile dog. He was a great patient to have as my first acupuncture case. He demonstrated to me the power of acupuncture. I finished my course, passed the qualifying written and practical tests, did the required case studies and internship, and became certified later the following year. I have continued to incorporate acupuncture into many of my cases to this day.

I've been a vet in practice now for forty years. I currently have two other veterinarians working for me. I have clients who have been with me since I started my practice in Arlington in 1981. I now have the pleasure and honor of having their children and even their children's children as clients. My practice has become my extended family.

During my career as a veterinarian, I have treated literally hundreds of thousands of animals, large and small. I have performed thousands of surgeries, including on a bear and a bald eagle. The time I have spent as a veterinarian has taught me much more than just the medical and surgical aspect of treating our animal friends with whose care we are entrusted. I have learned about life, love, loss, and resiliency.

As I look back on my career, I realize that being a veterinarian is not what I do but who I am. I made the decision as a twelve-year-old boy to embark on this path. I spent the next twelve years pursuing this goal. Then I endeavored through the next four decades as a professional in my field. My work has provided me with a noble purpose in life. Caring for God's creatures is what I was called to do. Through every tumultuous event in my life, my practice and my profession have been my rock. I know that without the support of my staff and all of my clients, I would not have survived the difficult times I have faced. It is this connection with clients and their animals that drives me. If I am blessed with good health, I see myself continuing in my practice well into my seventies. I derive so much pleasure and sense of accomplishment when I help animals. I feel I have been truly and abundantly blessed in my life's work.

6

BUILDING A FAMILY LIFE

D r. Keith was the vet I lived with when I first arrived in Cottage Grove at the beginning of my career. He was also the person who introduced me to my wife. One evening as we were relaxing and talking at his house after work, he mentioned a client of his, Susie. He told me he thought Susie and I would get along well together and he said he would introduce me to her next time she was in town and came into the clinic with her dog. I was intrigued with the idea of meeting her. I had finished veterinary school; I considered this a major milestone. I was alone. I had not considered marriage while I was in veterinary college as I did not want to complicate the already difficult job of my studies. But now I had reached a point in my life where I was considering the possibility that marriage might be the next life step.

In early July, Susie came into the clinic with her dog, Summer, a golden retriever. Dr. Keith introduced us, and Susie and I talked for a short while after I had finished examining Summer. I could imagine asking Susie out as it had been easy for us to carry on a conversation. She lived in Arlington, Washington where she was caretaking her parents' farm. She would come down every couple of weeks to Cottage Grove where her mom and dad now resided. I told her that next time she came down, it would be nice to get together. She agreed and said she would call.

A week later she was back in Cottage Grove and she contacted me. Dr. Keith had a barbecue at his house that Friday night and invited

Susie, so we could meet and talk in a relaxed atmosphere. We ate and drank, enjoying the evening and each other's company. Susie and I got along well, and we made plans to go for a motorcycle ride that weekend. On Sunday I picked up Susie at her parents' house and we went for an afternoon ride around the backcountry roads and through the farm country south of Cottage Grove. It was a great afternoon and we enjoyed spending time with each other. This became our preferred activity together.

Our relationship quickly progressed. Soon, Susie was coming down almost every weekend to spend time with me. Our relationship was carried on long-distance and that made our time together in person even more precious. When she was down in Cottage Grove, I would spend all of my free time with her: going on rides, taking her places, and drinking. She liked to dance and drink like I did.

My drinking continued in the same rhythm of abstinence during work or obligations and heavy drinking during periods absent of pressing responsibility. In other words, I obsessively worked or I obsessively drank.

We both missed each other when we were apart. I wanted to marry her. I could envision being with Susie on a farm raising children. One evening in April 1981, I proposed to Susie and she accepted. It was one of the most nerve-racking and exhilarating nights of my life. It was a short courtship of nine months, but I was sure that our future together would be great. Our engagement was even shorter. We decided that July 11, 1981, would be a good date for the wedding. We would have the wedding in Colorado because my large family was all there. We drove my old Dodge truck back to Colorado and her family flew there in her dad's airplane. After the wedding, Susie and I spent our honeymoon driving and camping around Colorado, Wyoming, and Montana.

I had left my Cottage Grove job before our wedding. So, upon our return to the West Coast after our honeymoon adventure, we began our life together as husband and wife. The decision to start my own practice in Arlington, Washington, was made, in part, because that was where Susie's family property was located.

A year after our wedding, Susie became pregnant with our first child. We were so excited. We both really wanted children. I loved children and to have one of my own would be a great blessing. Though I was just starting my vet practice and we had no savings, I believed everything would fall into place. I knew I could provide for my family and I had all the love a child would need. I was going to be a dad!

When we went in for our first ultrasound, we saw the heartbeat contained in the small little body that was developing. We were excited to see our baby for the very first time. The ultrasound technician didn't say anything. But I sensed she was concerned about something as she repeatedly measured the baby's head. Our doctor came in and explained that there were some indicators of problems with our baby, and he advised us to go to Seattle to see a neonatal specialist. Naturally, we were quite worried. After our first exam and tests with the specialists, though, our fears were relieved; our baby did have a slightly enlarged head but the mild enlargement was within the normal range. I told my wife we needed to celebrate, so I found a nice restaurant and we had a relaxing dinner. A giant weight had been lifted off our shoulders. We giggled excitedly as we drove north up the interstate to our home in Arlington and imagined what life would be like with this new baby.

We had a number of follow-up exams, ultrasounds, and consultations over the course of the next several months. But in the fifth month of pregnancy, everything dramatically changed. The specialist we had been working with told us that our baby had multiple severe conditions, including hydrocephalus and a serious heart defect. We were advised to travel to Denver where we would be treated by nationally renowned neonatal specialists. Susie and I were devastated. I closed my veterinary practice for a week while we traveled to Colorado. We were faced with so many uncertainties. We had no idea what type of outcome we were facing with our precious little baby. All we could do is hope and pray for the best.

The team of specialists who shepherded us through this ordeal were kind and caring. They spent the first day and a half running tests. The next day we were called in to a conference of too many doctors who weren't smiling when we walked in. They were compassionate as they explained our daughter's problems. Our baby's condition was not treatable and she would never survive birth. There was absolutely nothing the specialist doctors could do to save our baby. Further, we were told that Susie's life was at risk if the pregnancy continued. This was incomprehensibly horrifying news. Any hope that had traveled with us on the plane from Seattle to Denver was gone. Our dreams for our baby were utterly destroyed.

We were left with absolutely no choice. That evening we went into the hospital in preparation for them to induce labor early the next morning. We cried together. There was so much we couldn't fathom or understand. We talked for a long time about our baby. We felt she needed a name, so we decided on "Abby." Early the next morning, they induced labor. It took three excruciating days of contractions and painful emotions for Susie to deliver Abby. I ushered in nurses to administer pain meds, cried, held and supported Susie, and occasionally collapsed into the chair at her bedside. Finally, after seventy-two hours of pure hell, Abby was born.

There was no crying of a newborn infant to make all the pain of labor worth the effort. Abby had died during birth. There was only somber silence filling the hospital room. It was like a tomb: Abby's tomb. Susie lay back in her bed, soaked in sweat and despondent beyond measure. They gave her medication to relax and to help with her pain. I asked them to give Abby to me. I needed to hold our baby. Then they left us alone to grieve.

I showed Abby to Susie. She held our daughter for a few minutes until the medications they had given her took over and she fell asleep for the first time in days. I sat with Abby in my arms. I looked down at her. She fit in the palms of my hands, weighing a minute one and a half pounds. She had a full head of black hair and brown eyes. She was purple, wrinkled, cold. And she was beautiful, my daughter. I loved her more than I knew I could love somebody. I held Abby and talked to her as I wept. I told my baby that I loved her. I asked her to go find my grandparents and my friends, Vern and Dave. They would take care of her in heaven. I told Abby to watch over us and to wait for me in heaven. I said that I missed her, and I held her close against my chest. I baptized Abby, taking water from my glass and blessing her with the sign of the cross over her tiny, delicate forehead. I quietly said, "I bless you in the name of the Father, and of the Son, and of the Holy Ghost." I didn't know what else to do or say. It was a moment beyond words.

I held Abby for about an hour. I could feel her getting colder, but I could not let her go. I just stared at her beautiful face. I thought about how I would never change her diaper, never sing her a goodnight lullaby, never watch her crawl. I would never see her first step, never hold her on my lap, never help her with schoolwork. I would never hang up a Christmas stocking for her, never get her a puppy or kitten, never walk holding her small hand in mine. I thought about how I would not see her grow up into a woman. I thought these things and more. I felt the tears well up in my eyes and flow down my face, falling onto her body. These were tears I had not allowed myself to shed before this moment because I had to be strong for Susie. But now my wife was asleep and I was alone with Abby. My tears continued to rain down onto Abby. I felt she would understand. I loved Abby.

After a time, the nurse came and gently lifted Abby from my arms. I did not want to see her go. I did not know what to do and I did not know how to feel. I was numb with grief. I could not make any sense of what had happened or why. I was lost. I was not sure I could even survive, but I knew I had to. Susie needed me. I had felt powerless during this ordeal: ashamed that I could not do more, ashamed that all my medical knowledge hadn't helped us save Abby. Now I had to help Susie deal with our loss and heal as much as possible. That night, I sat in the chair next to Susie's bed. I did not sleep. Whenever she woke up, I consoled her.

The next day was tear-filled as our team of doctors and nurses—those compassionate specialists who had been with us throughout our entire stay—hugged us and told us how sad they were as they shared our loss. They had been phenomenal with their wealth of medical and emotional support. We flew back home with heavy hearts.

I had to go back to work immediately. Our trip to Denver and the associated medical expenses had wiped out our savings. I tried to help Susie deal with her grief even as I struggled to deal with my own. We would talk about Abby. We would go outside on our farm and look up at the night sky, saying one of the stars in heaven was our baby looking over us. It was hard to talk to anyone else about my grief. Some people didn't understand how losing a stillborn baby could be so painful; others told me everything would be fine and that I should just move on. Finally, I quit talking about my pain. Instead, I drank in an attempt to ease an unbearable, and unfixable, agony. But it never totally subsided and Abby has never left my heart. I think about her and still talk to her. I hope she loves her dad and is saving me a spot in heaven next to her and all those I've loved who have gone before me. I know that my precious daughter Abby is my angel in heaven.

Susie and I felt an indescribable chasm of emptiness inside of us and inside of our house. The nursery we had started remained empty, as did her crib. There was no baby to fill our hearts or our house.

Over time, as we tried to come to terms with our loss, we reached a point where we both felt Abby would want to be a big sister. We felt that she deserved to have siblings to watch over from her place in heaven. Abby would be able to guide them as their guardian angel.

Susie was scared to bear another pregnancy and I understood, sharing her fear. We decided adoption would be a good way to start a family. The first step in adopting was to do a home study—the process to ensure we would be good parents and that our home would be a healthy one for raising children. The home study was an extensive process over three months that included background checks; letters of recommendation from friends, our priest, my colleagues; a tax return and financial review; and interviews, questionnaires, and observations of us in our home.

In the spring of 1983, my oldest brother called from Nebraska and said he knew a couple who wanted to put their unborn baby up for adoption to a good home. On June 24th we received the call; we were the proud parents of a healthy baby boy. We flew to Omaha to pick him up. The very instant I held my newborn son in my arms, gazing down at this amazing little human, I felt the overwhelming love of a father. I tenderly held Cody's miniature hands in mine. Like all first-time parents, we doted on our child. But due to the trauma we had experienced with Abby, we were more apprehensive; we hovered over Cody when anything happened. To us, he was a miracle. When Cody was a year and half old, we decided it was time to give him some siblings and to grow our family; we always knew we wanted lots of children.

It took more than a year and a half to be placed with a Korean baby. In June 1986, we became the proud parents of a beautiful baby girl, Kelly, who had been born a month earlier. Kelly could not be flown over to us until she was three or four months old, so we prepared her nursery as we eagerly awaited her arrival. In September, we traveled to Sea-Tac Airport to meet the volunteer who had flown from Korea with Kelly. I picked up this perfectly formed baby with chubby cheeks and a big smile, and once more felt the swell of fatherly love and connection with my beautiful daughter.

At about this same time, Susie's parents decided to sell their farm. They were dividing it up and so I made an offer for the front section, which had about thirty-five acres. It included the old farmhouse and numerous barns. I also bought all of their farming equipment and a small herd of Scotch Highland cattle. We were thrilled. Susie and I both loved the farm and thought it was the ideal place to raise children. We sold the ten-acre parcel we'd been living on and moved back over to

Susie's parents' (now *our*) property. I finally had the small farm of my dreams.

There was a span of three years between Cody and Kelly. Susie and I thought it would be nice to adopt a child who would fall in between their ages. We once more contacted Catholic Community Services, which had helped us with Kelly. They placed us with Bo Mee, a two-and-half-year-old girl from an orphanage in Seoul. She seemed like the perfect match for us.

The adoption of our third child coincided with the Olympic Games being held in Seoul, Korea. We were contacted by KING 5 TV in Seattle, which was doing a weeklong series highlighting South Korea, and they wanted to do a human interest story on our family's Korean adoptions. Jean Enersen, one of the most highly recognized and well-regarded news anchors in the Pacific Northwest, visited the orphanage in Seoul and filmed the children there. She paid particular attention to our daughter, Bo Mee. Jean then came up to our farmhouse after she returned from Korea and showed us the footage they had taken at the orphanage. She filmed our family in Arlington while we watched the video, capturing our excitement as we got a few moving glimpses of the daughter we had not yet met in person. We were overjoyed to see our daughter walking around the orphanage and playing with the other children wearing a giant smile on her face. She was truly beautiful.

In early November, Bo Mee and twenty other adopted Korean children were flown to Sea-Tac Airport. Of course, we were waiting there to greet her. KING 5 TV and the *Everett Herald* (our county newspaper) were both at the airport to film the momentous occasion for the stories they were running on us. They chronicled for the world such an incredibly happy moment for our family; Bo Mee, exhausted from her transatlantic flight, and still dressed in her heavy red-plaid, two-piece pajamas, was placed in my arms. They had forgotten her shoes on the plane, so she only had white socks on her feet.

The *Everett Herald* featured us on the front page as a Thanksgiving story and KING 5 TV had featured the first part of our story during the week of the Olympic Games. Jean Enersen also did an end-of-the-year special where she replayed her favorite stories of 1988 and we were featured in her special. These stories helped capture a magical time in our family's growth and I cherish the memories they help preserve.

The following summer, Susie came up to the barn where I was working on a sunny Saturday morning and announced that she was pregnant. I immediately felt elated as well as apprehensive; we had been through hell with the loss of our first biological child. But many doctor appointments and reassurances later, we were blessed with a healthy, beautiful baby girl, Noel. I was the first person to hold her and I did not want to ever put her down. She was a completely healthy baby. I loved her instantly. It was such a profound moment, just as the arrival of each of my first three children had been. Our baby's three siblings were in awe of Noel and could not get enough opportunities to gently touch her tiny features.

Our children grew, and three years later Susie again brought me news that she was pregnant. This time we were blessed with another beautiful baby girl, Mariah. I assisted with the delivery and viewed her birth as a miracle. When the obstetrician handed me my fourth daughter (and fifth child), I was overcome with emotion. I could hardly breathe I was so happy. All I wanted to do was sit and hold Mariah's tiny body and to stare at her in wonder. Sitting and rocking my children always soothed my soul and provided me with deep peace.

A couple of years later, we were contacted by a friend who had heard about a very young African American girl in Pennsylvania who was pregnant. We had a family meeting and discussed the situation with our children, and we all agreed that we could provide a loving home for another baby. We moved forward with the process. On March 12, 1996, our little boy Isaiah was born in Philadelphia. Susie and our oldest son flew out to welcome Isaiah into our family and to bring him home. Once more, I felt the powerful love and protective instincts of a father immediately well up inside of me the moment I took my youngest child into my arms at the airport. He was a handsome baby boy.

Our family was now complete. We had six children: two boys and four girls. Two of our children were "homemade." Four were adopted. Three were Caucasian, two were Korean, and one was African American. We truly raised a mix of God's children.

My kids enjoyed helping me on our farm. They learned at a young age how to drive the tractor and old farm truck, so they could drive while the rest of us picked up the hay bales after I had mowed our largest pasture. They helped build fences as well as feed and work with the animals on the farm. Often, one of the younger children would fall asleep while I was working out on the farm and I would find them nestled in the front seat of the old farm truck. I loved spending time on the farm with my children.

Life on our farm was not all work. We had a swimming pool where the children spent summer days swimming and diving. We usually ate on the patio around the pool, barbecuing most warm evenings. When the kids weren't swimming, they could be found on our playground. It included a large sandbox, trampoline, and a three-story play structure I had built. The tower had an enclosed room on the top level, two slides—a circular, enclosed one and another one that was undulating—three swings, and a climbing area. The children also loved to explore the natural areas on our farm, going down to the pond or up into the woods. No matter where they went, there was always a caravan of dogs following. Our house had a very large playroom in the basement that contained a miniature kitchen built to scale; I recall many times sitting at the child-sized table on a tiny chair sipping "tea" with my girls. It had ten-foot-high walls so we set up a small basketball hoop, and the kids could also roller skate on the heated cement floor.

I loved taking my children to my vet clinic and having them see all the animals. I enjoyed having them watch me care for my patients.

When I had weekend emergency calls, I would often take one or two of my children with me to the clinic or out to the farms where the emergency was taking place. They enjoyed being with me and being around all the animals. As they got older, they would help me at vaccination clinics, hand me equipment on farm calls, and do cleaning at the clinic. I remember when Cody was two and I would put him on the counter as I was examining animals. I would turn around and find him eating Pet Tabs from the treat jar. My children would watch me do surgeries from the time they were three or four. I remember Mariah coming into the clinic from the time she was a preschooler and pulling up a step stool next to my treatment table to watch me doing minor surgeries. My children remember watching me do surgery on a bear, and later on a bald eagle. They loved seeing the baby animals and helping with C-sections. It instilled in my children a love for animals that they carry with them to this day.

Our family celebrated all of the major holidays, but Christmas was an especially cherished time for us. The excitement started the week prior to Thanksgiving and grew in intensity as Christmas approached. Each child would hint about what they wanted or give us a list. Homemade gifts were an important part of Christmas for me. I wanted my children to have things I made for them long after I am gone. I would start working in my shop the weekend after Thanksgiving; the family knew not to come up uninvited into "Santa's Shop." The mini kitchen in our basement was one of those presents that came out of my shop at Christmastime. On several occasions, a close friend of mine dressed up as Santa and visited the farm a few days prior to Christmas. My kids loved his visits and still talk about it. All of this preparation led up to exuberant excitement and chaos as the children opened presents from family on Christmas Eve. Then, after a sleepless night, they would rush downstairs when we called up the steps, "Okay, you can come down now." Their stockings were hung on the fireplace mantel and I would fill each one with a toothbrush, tangerine, small presents, and candy—

just how my stocking was filled when I was a child. Then my children would open presents from Santa. Their joy and laughter made all of our planning worthwhile.

My life seemed to be a fulfillment of the dream I had when I was young. I was approaching forty years of age, had a large family on a picturesque farm full of animals, and a veterinary clinic where I practiced the profession to which I was passionately called. I loved caring for my children, working the property, and tending the animals both on my farm and at my clinic. My farm contained everything I needed, including an old chicken coop that I had converted into a woodworking shop. In short, I was enthralled with my work as a vet, my beautiful and loving children, the menagerie of animals around us, and the gorgeous land on which we all resided.

But deep down inside, I knew there were problems with my relationship with my wife. I never thought of them as insurmountable; I believed they were a normal part of raising a family with lots of kids and responsibilities. And I hoped that they would pass with time and effort.

I rarely drank at home, and when I did I had only a beer or two. But sometimes when my relationship with my wife was especially intense, I would stop after work for several drinks with a client or at a bar. Occasionally, I would go home drunk. It was my dysfunctional method of delaying or buffering what I was increasingly experiencing with Susie. Our relationship lacked intimacy both physically and emotionally. We continually argued about money, child raising, and how to divvy up the house and farm chores. It seemed like an endless downward spiral for our marriage.

7

HOUSE FIRE

Our family had outgrown our old farmhouse. Susie and I started plans for a new house that would easily accommodate all of us. We could envision our new home sitting just east of the old farmhouse in the pasture. We had installed an inground pool years before, with the thought that our home would go next to it. I wanted to wait to build until I had a significant amount of savings so I would not have to borrow so much.

When I awoke one Sunday morning in August 1995, I had no inkling that the events that were about to unfold would tragically alter the course I was on.

It was one of those ideal summer days in the Pacific Northwest: sunny, mid-80s, not a cloud in the blue sky, and a slight breeze to freshen the air. I wanted to enjoy the morning with a horseback ride in our north pasture. I knew that my youngest daughter Mariah, at two and a half, would enjoy riding with me. I had taken her before—sitting in front of me on the saddle—and she had enjoyed it. We had been gently riding for about twenty minutes when I heard a single lightning strike in the distance behind me, south toward Everett. This surprised me on such a clear day. I immediately turned my quarter horse around; I didn't want to be out with my daughter during a lightning storm. As I was heading back to the house, I saw smoke coming out from under the eaves on both sides of our home. It took me a minute to realize what this signified. My first thought was, *Weird, it's summer. We don't have*

59

a fire going in the fireplace. Next, *We aren't barbecuing today.* These two thoughts were instantaneous and automatic. Then, like a bullet, it hit me. Our home was on fire! What if my wife and other children were in the house? I had to get back.

I pushed my horse into a gallop; I was trying to balance my daughter's safety—as I held her tightly to my chest—with the panic for my other children that was welling up inside of me. We covered the distance to home rapidly and I came to an abrupt stop at the corral. I quickly dismounted with Mariah and left our still-saddled horse in the corral. As I ran to the front yard, I saw my wife and the other children outside in our large garden across the driveway from our home. They were picking flowers about a hundred feet from the house. My wife and children had their backs to the house and were oblivious to the smoke behind them. I thanked God that they were all safe. I shouted to everyone, "The house is on fire!" I gathered up the children, putting them and our little dogs in the cab of my pickup truck to keep them safe. I secured the big dogs in the bed of the pickup.

I yelled again to my wife. "The house is on fire! Call 9-1-1!"

I ran into the house and could smell and see the smoke hanging in the air as I dashed upstairs. Turning the corner, I could see smoke billowing out under the door to our oldest girls' room. I ran back outside, grabbed a garden hose, and headed back up. This time as I turned that corner at the top of the stairs, the force of the fire hit me like a sledgehammer and pushed me back against the wall. I dropped the hose, stumbling down the stairs and back outside.

The volunteer fire department showed up within fifteen minutes, but it seemed like an eternity. Three pump-ladder trucks and one tanker truck initially arrived along with the fire chief's vehicle. The tanker truck was the sole source of water for putting out the fire. They quickly started to fight the fire. Smoke was now billowing out of every open window and the door. After fifteen minutes, they called for another tanker truck since they were already running low on water. It was difficult to get the second tanker truck close enough as the narrow driveway was clogged with all the vehicles. Two firemen carried a ladder to the house and climbed up on the roof so they could cut a hole in it, but their chainsaw would not start. I grabbed my Stihl chainsaw and handed it up to one of the firemen. They cut the hole and proceeded to fight the fire from the ground as well as from the roof.

As this mayhem ensued, two of our little dogs escaped from the truck and ran back into the house. I tried to go back in to get them but the firemen would not allow me to enter through the front door. I had to get our dogs. I went around to a back window that opened into the living room. I pushed it open and climbed into the house. I dropped to the floor with the chokingly thick smoke. I couldn't see anything through the haze. I tried to think about where two scared little dogs might hide. I pictured them huddled behind our couch. Praying I was right, I felt my way across the living room to the couch. I moved it away from the wall and crawled in behind it. I reached out and touched one dog, and then the other. I thanked God again as I crawled back with the dogs cradled under one arm. It was all I could do to make it to the window as my eyes and lungs were burning from the heavy smoke and heat. Holding the dogs, I rolled out of the window onto the rhododendron bush below. I just lay there for a minute, exhausted and gasping for breath. The smoke grew darker as it poured from the window I had just exited. I went back to the truck where my children were crying, worried about me, their dogs, and their home. We hugged, and then all we could do was sit there while the fire gutted our house. For the next two hours, we watched in horror as the firemen battled the blaze. We were stranded as our driveway remained blocked with fire trucks.

Finally, the firefighters determined that all of the embers had been extinguished. Many of those volunteer firefighters were friends and clients. They came and offered their support and sympathy. They did not know what to say. We were numb. It is a terrible feeling to be homeless, especially with young kids. I tried to comfort my wife and children, telling them we would make it through and that we needed to be thankful that no life was lost. But I kept to myself just how scared I was about being able to work through this enormous ordeal. I felt an overwhelming sense of loss. I could not fully process what had just happened. But I knew I had a family to care for. Our closest neighbors offered their basement as temporary shelter. It was a welcome refuge. They fed us dinner; we hadn't eaten all day. Then we laid out pads on the cement floor and fell into a fitful sleep. I had ongoing nightmares of the fire. I could still feel the heat and smell the smoke. In some of the dreams, I was horrified that I hadn't saved the dogs and they had died. In other nightmares, my children were trapped in the fire. I kept waking up in a sweat, disoriented. I would look around at my family sprawled across the floor and say yet another prayer of gratitude that I hadn't lost a child.

The next morning, I awoke before daybreak and walked through the woods to our house. What an eerie sight those charred remains were as the first light of day fell on the carcass of a house. The walls were still intact, but were covered in soot and water. The large gaping hole in the center of the roof looked at me like an evil cyclops. The roof sagged. I slowly walked in a trance across the porch and into the house. It was completely surreal. Where only twenty-four hours before my family had been eating breakfast, now there was no life at all. The thick, acrid smell of smoke mixed with the moist water vapor assaulted my nose and burned my eyes. The only sound was water dripping. Tiles littered the floor or hung precariously from the exposed wood that had once been our ceiling. The floor was a puddle of black water and debris. Cabinet doors hung haphazardly.

I slowly made my way into the living room and then into our bedrooms on the ground floor. Smoke and water had damaged every surface. I walked upstairs to the very place that I had been repelled in my vain attempt to save our home; the garden hose now lay there inert in the stairwell. Looking at that small green hose, I realized how futile my actions had been. The upstairs was where the force of the inferno produced the most damage. I walked through the girls' rooms where their beds, clothes, and toys were ruined. Next to their bedroom was our attic, where the fire had originated. One of the first things I noticed was that all of our Christmas decorations had been reduced to a pile of ash, including all of the handmade decorations my children had made over the years. All of these precious keepsakes were gone; only the memories of them remained. Through the hole in the roof, I could see the soft morning light. It was a stark contrast to the reality that lay within. I stood there staring in shock, dazed by what had happened to my family's home, and worried about what lay ahead of us.

The children were already enrolled in a weeklong horseback riding camp along with the daughter of the friends with whom we were staying. We discussed whether or not they should go, after what had happened. What is best for children after they lose their home cannot be found in any parenting manual. We decided they should go. It would help take their minds off the fire. We felt it was a blessing that our children had a scheduled activity to help them get back into the flow of life. So that week, while I worked to restore our lives to some sort of equilibrium, they spent the days horseback riding through the woods.

I took off that entire week from work. The fire marshal came out. Based on the burn pattern, he located where the fire originated. He showed me an electrical wire that he said was the cause of the fire. He mentioned that occasionally there can be defects in the wire or that rodents sometimes chew them. Three insurance adjusters also came out that week to survey the damage and discuss with us the process for navigating this ordeal. They would work with us to provide temporary housing and meals, pay the maximum of our policy to repair the house, and determine the value of our lost possessions. We learned that we could put our settlement toward the new house we had been planning to build instead of trying to gut and rebuild the old one.

Time passed in a blur. Friends came on the weekends to help. I took sole responsibility for picking through the house and seeing what could be saved. When I wasn't at the clinic working, I would be at the house going through the wreckage. The summer days were long and I spent the daylight hours salvaging or disposing of what had been our life's possessions. At the end of each night, I had to take a long shower to get the smell of smoke off my body. My life became work, the fire, and recovery from the fire. We had rented a huge dumpster to hold the debris from our wrecked house; the overflowing receptacle had to be emptied several times. One Sunday about three weeks after the fire—and two days after my fortieth birthday—I was sitting on the top edge of the dirty dumpster. I looked inside the dumpster at our ruined possessions. I looked at the yard and saw more of our ruined possessions strewn about on the lawn. And I cried. I was mentally and physically exhausted. Yet, I had no choice but to continue picking through the rubble. I had no choice but to continue trying to save any object that could help us remember life's important moments. We had lost so much that the few remaining items became invaluable.

After a couple of weeks staying with our neighbors, we moved into an old motel nearby. We lived in three adjoining rooms on the second floor. The novelty helped our children for a short while, but soon it became monotonous. It was difficult to live this way. We had to buy new clothes for everyone, including new school uniforms for the girls. We had cold cereal every morning and would eat out for lunch and dinner. We had to take our clothes to the laundromat. It was impossible to stay organized. Life was hectic and out of balance. This was to be our home and how we would live for several months.

All the while, I prepared a spot on our farm to hook up a trailer. I laid a gravel pad, hooked up utilities, and cut a driveway into the pasture. The weekend after Thanksgiving—four months after our house and the sum total of our material possessions burned up—we moved from the motel to our double-wide modular shelter on our property. The thousand-square-foot trailer was very crowded for eight people, six dogs, and four cats. This trailer was going to be our home for the next eighteen months while we designed and built our new house. We wanted to make the best of a very tragic situation. So, we decided to see and learn as much as we could about designing a dream house from the ashes of a nightmare. We went to a number of home shows as well as toured custom-built houses. We visited area kitchen, bath, and home improvement stores for ideas. I read voraciously and researched geothermal heating systems, air exchange systems, heated floors, and all of the other components of a high-end house. We traveled far to look at homes that were built in sections. They were beautiful. We finally found a model that we loved and that we knew would suit our family perfectly.

With my extensive background in construction—six summers and numerous breaks from college building custom homes, doing major remodels, and building custom cabinets under the tutelage of an expert carpenter—I decided to be the general contractor on our new house project. It took three months to get the plans approved and to receive our building permit. We started building in the late winter, not the best time in the Pacific Northwest. I had done some preliminary site preparation with a backhoe I had on the farm. The real work started when I rented a large track hoe for two weeks; a friend operated the machine and dug the hole for our house. We located the house in our pasture next to the inground swimming pool we had installed three years prior. It was an idyllic setting.

I put in a full, insulated basement with ten-foot-high walls. I used stacking, Styrofoam blocks into which I poured cement. I put up the blocks with the help of friends who would come over to assist. It was actually quite fun: a giant Lego project that my children loved. I then worked with a crew to frame the main floor and the upstairs. Each child would have their own room. Five bathrooms instead of the two we had all shared in the farmhouse. I continued to work full-time at the clinic. But on my days off as well as every evening, I would work on the house. I coordinated and oversaw the entire process, as well as labored with the construction crew when I could. Each morning before work, I would get the crew organized. Occasionally at lunch, I would run home to see how things were progressing. There were never-ending decisions to make.

We had a new well drilled. The driller "witched" to find the best spot to drill and told me that there was good water at ninety feet below the soil surface. One of the Seattle television stations came up and filmed him. They were doing a story on well witching. Though I thought it was bogus, I was instructed in how to hold the copper wire and—despite not wanting it to work—the wire actually moved, indicating where the underground water existed. This occurred three times over the same spot. This was mind-boggling for me: a scientifically trained, empirically oriented veterinarian. The well-digger drilled in the designated spot. At ninety-two feet, we hit clear, clean water in great abundance; it squirted up out of the Earth when the digger reached the aquifer. I was in total shock; it was just one more thing in life I did not understand. But I was happy and relieved that it worked.

One morning when we were already well into the framing of our house, I stepped back and tripped over a large beam. The pneumatic nailer in my hand hit the outside of my right knee. It drove a two-and-a-half-inch nail through my knee. Thankfully, it missed the bone. The nail stuck out from both sides of my pants. I reached down and pulled out the nail. The other three men stopped and stared. I went inside and cleaned the wounds. I had lunch, rested for an hour, and went back to work for the rest of the day. It was a miracle no damage was done.

The framing was finally finished and the plumbers, electricians, and other tradesmen descended on the house to install the myriad of components that make a house function. As the tradesmen plied their crafts, I started designing and building the cabinets for the kitchen and bathrooms. I made the cabinets in my shop: the old chicken shed with a seven-foot ceiling and no windows. I spent most nights working there until two in the morning building cabinets. It was tiring but also quite rewarding to see my ideas come to life.

Once the interior was painted, the finish work started. I was fortunate to have a friend, Mike, work for me trimming out the house. He is the best finish carpenter I have ever seen. With him, I underwent my second apprenticeship in woodworking. We put in crown molding, milling most of our finish wood right in the house. We stained, finished, and installed trim around the doors, windows, and baseboard. My friend transformed our master bedroom and bathroom into a masterpiece. Working with Mike was quite rewarding; he was a true master of his craft.

I spent the rest of my time in the shop working on the cabinets. The large kitchen came together just as I had envisioned it. I made elegant doors and drawer fronts out of locally sourced alder and maple; I applied a clear finish that allowed the beauty of the wood to shine through. I laid Pergo floors in the kitchen and dining area. It was a beautiful and very functional kitchen. For the bathroom cabinets I made doors and drawer fronts with Formica surfaces wrapped with quarter-inch oak trim. They looked bright, crisp, and clean. I felt great satisfaction when I looked at my finished cabinets.

After all of my effort, and the ongoing labor of numerous workers, our new house was finally completed.

We were very excited to move out of the tiny trailer just prior to Thanksgiving. The first night we all lay on the carpeted floor of our great room. We looked up into the great expanse of the twenty-four-foot ceiling overhead and laughed. That first night in our new home was phenomenal. We got our six children into beds, each in their very own bedroom. Our dream home had become a reality. I expected that this would be our home forever: that our children would grow up here, and in time their children would come to stay and play. I felt at home. I felt at peace.

Our first Christmas in the house, we all went out to a local tree farm and cut down the biggest tree we thought would fit in our great room. It was eighteen feet tall and we could barely get it through the door. I put it in a heavy-duty Christmas tree stand. We had so much fun decorating it from top to bottom, using a large ladder to reach the top to put on the star. A few days later, I was having my early morning coffee at the kitchen counter. Out of the corner of my eye I caught the blur of one of our young cats; she was dashing through the living room and ran straight up to the top of the tree. What happened next seemed to occur in slow motion. The tree started swaying. By the time I rushed over, the tree was well on its way to the ground. I couldn't stop it, so I just watched. The tree hit the floor and the cat bolted out the top across the star. The cat was as shocked as I was. I had to laugh at how comical it was. When the rest of the family woke up, we worked to get the tree righted. A few glass ornaments had broken but overall the tree was unscathed. I learned my lesson and stabilized the top of the tree with wires attached to the walls. It made our first Christmas memorable and funny. There are very few things I like more than spending Christmas with my family and this was a special Christmas, indeed, in our new home. We were finally home.

8

DIVORCE

Over the years, my relationship with Susie had continued to deteriorate. We were not close, and Susie seemed distant. I would talk to her about this change and she would tell me I was just too sensitive and that she was fine. She said she was just busy with the children. I felt more and more isolated. It was weird, being so lonely when I was married. The many life changes we were experiencing—frequent moves, starting my own practice, and beginning a family—seemed to me to be understandable reasons for a shift in our relationship. But I also noticed patterns evolving that I did not like: financial issues, intimacy problems, and unresolved grief from the loss of our first baby Abby. Our one shared activity continued to be our drinking.

Susie's spending increased and she seemed to always want "one more thing" to make her happy. She started writing checks from both our personal and business accounts and it became impossible to make a budget or build up a savings account. It was all I could do to make enough money to cover normal expenses plus her spending. When I tried to discuss financial matters with her, she would say I spent a lot at work and she felt she could spend a lot too. I explained that those were actual business expenses necessary to run my vet practice. I would bring home all of my records to show her so she could understand. But she continued to overspend.

Our relationship continued to get worse and I increasingly dreaded going home after work. I loved seeing my children and spending time with them, but I knew that as soon as I would walk through the door Susie would start telling me how bad her day was. I was never able to calm her. In a short time, an argument would ensue. This is when I began occasionally stopping for a couple of beers to stall the scene that played out incessantly upon my return home. I knew I needed to stay in the marriage for my children; I felt it was my duty as a father to do whatever I could to make their childhood as good as possible. I just did not know how long I could continue to be in so much pain and loneliness.

By the summer of 1999, after eighteen years of marriage, six children, and all we had built, our marriage had deteriorated to a degree that was extraordinarily hard on Susie, me, and the children. We did not get along as a couple or as parents. We shared few activities and almost no intimacy. We constantly fought about money. I also fought with Susie because I felt she treated the children unfairly. She thought I paid too much attention to our kids and not enough to her. I decided a divorce was the only answer. I talked to Susie, expressing my pain, and told her that I wanted a divorce. I had not viewed divorce as an option for many years because of my Catholic upbringing.

Susie implored me to try to work things out, and I agreed for the sake of the children. We enrolled in an extensive marriage intervention program where we spent two weekends at a retreat, and then had monthly, day-long sessions in which we worked on communication and understanding skills. I felt that with both of us working on these skills, there was a chance we could save our relationship and have the marriage about which I had always dreamed. My hope was that we could become a true partnership: close, intimate parents unified in raising our children.

It was during this time of working to salvage our marriage that Susie started to spend more time away from home. The children would call me at work asking where their mom was and what was for dinner. I told them I didn't know where she was and that I would plan what to do for dinner, either picking up food or going home and cooking for them.

Some evenings Susie wouldn't come home until nine or ten o'clock after I had the children in bed. When I asked her where she had been, she said she had been with a friend who was helping her "find" herself and work to become a better person. They would attend women's workshops overnight in Seattle together. She said it went along with the work we were doing on our marriage.

On a Monday several months later, a friend who had been a client for nearly seventeen years came in to my clinic and asked to talk with me privately. We went into a quiet room and she told me that a mutual acquaintance had told her that Susie was frequenting bars, getting drunk and wild, and having an affair. I did not want to believe it. Susie and I were working on our marriage. I told my friend that I needed to talk directly to our mutual acquaintance. The next day I spoke on the phone with this acquaintance, someone I had known for several years. She described how Susie would leave the children alone all day and go see a man who lived in the next town. This acquaintance gave me a rough idea of where this man lived.

The next day I got in my car during a break in my workday. I drove to the neighborhood the acquaintance described as the one in which the man lived. As I drove down a street, I saw Susie's Mustang parked in a driveway. As I passed by, Susie and a man I assumed to be her lover came out of the house near her car and saw me driving by. I returned to my clinic shaken, not believing what I had just seen. A few minutes later, Susie burst in and started yelling incoherently at me. "How could you follow me? It is none of your business. He and I are just friends." She went on and on. I listened to her and then simply said, "We are done." Susie did not come home that night. I fed the children and put them to bed. I was heartbroken; every dream I had was crushed. My children asked where their mom was, but all I could say was that I did not know. The next day Susie returned and made all sorts of promises to change her behavior. But time and experience had shown me that nothing would change.

Later that week, Susie and my daughter had made plans for an out-of-town birthday weekend. But as I lay in bed the night they left, I was overcome with a powerful sense that Susie had taken our daughter to her lover's house instead of to the hotel I'd booked for their special weekend. I tossed and turned all night, worried about my daughter. Finally, at about five in the morning, I decided the only way I could resolve this was to go back to the man's house. I hoped beyond hope that I would not find them there, that Susie's Mustang would not be in her lover's driveway again. I did not want my children subjected to that kind of immoral activity. But, devastatingly, I found my wife's car at his house. I was immediately filled with angst. I took my daughter back to the safety of home. That afternoon, Susie came home with some friends and began to yell at me about retrieving our daughter. We got into a shouting match and she went outside to call the sheriff over to our house. The sheriff told us that one of us had to leave. No one was arrested as there was no sign of physical altercation. Susie left. We did not see her for a week.

That evening I called a mutual friend to let her know what was happening. She told me that she knew about Susie's affair. I also phoned several other friends of Susie and each one corroborated the previous facts I had been told, adding more details to the story of a life Susie was living about which I knew nothing. All of these conversations weighed heavily on me. I was an emotional wreck.

A few nights later, around two thirty in the morning, I heard a loud knocking on the door. Two deputies were standing there and told me I had ten minutes to leave my home, that Susie had filed assault charges against me. I told them I could not leave as I had five children sleeping in the house; at that point, my children ranged in age from sixteen down to four years old. The sheriffs told me they did not care and that my children being all alone was not their concern; their only job was to evict me from my home. I had to leave immediately. I protested again about leaving my children by themselves, but the sheriffs were unrelenting. Very reluctantly, I got dressed and left. I was in total shock. I posed no danger to anyone and my children would be left totally alone. I drove to my clinic and went upstairs to my office. I would not see or hear from my children for the next two weeks. Those were two of the most agonizing weeks of my life, as I was separated from my children and overwhelmingly concerned for their safety.

But finally, I was granted visitation rights on Wednesday evenings and weekends. Susie would have our children the rest of the time. It was decided that neither Susie or I would permanently live at the house; the children would reside in our family home and we would take turns staying there during our designated visitation times. I continued to sleep in my office at the clinic when it was Susie's turn with the children; Susie stayed with her mom or at her lover's house when I was at home with our children. I tried to make my time with my children as normal as possible, playing with them during the summer days. Being with them was what gave me purpose and kept me fighting for custody.

During this time, Susie—in her rage at the situation—made repeated accusations about how I fathered our children. It took every bit of stamina to continually counter her false claims. This muddied the situation unnecessarily and took a great toll on me that I would only later understand. On one occasion as the divorce proceeded, Susie became enraged with our oldest daughter and began to choke her. I rushed my daughter to the emergency room, hopeful that this incident of Susie's would bring an end to the craziness of false allegations against me. But it changed nothing. The shared custody and divorce proceedings were continually exasperating to me. From the day she was choked, my oldest daughter lived with me at the clinic during the week and at home with me when I had weekend visitations.

As part of the divorce conditions, the court required that Susie and I attend a parenting seminar in Everett. I signed up to attend the seminar on a Saturday. The court made a point of saying that in order to receive credit for the seminar, I could not be late. If I did not attend, I would lose my custody rights. I woke up early the morning of the seminar in order to do the many farm chores before having to leave. When I walked outside to leave, I found that both my truck and Suburban had four flat tires each and the valve stems had been bent or jammed with wood to ruin them. I would be unable to simply fill them with air and drive to the seminar. I saw that whoever had vandalized my cars had brought up large soup bones to give to the dogs to keep them quiet. I panicked for a minute, until I realized that my neighbor might lend me his car for the day. He kindly did so. I barely made it to my court-mandated seminar on time. But fortunately, I did; I would not lose my custody rights over someone else's malicious intent.

Another part of the divorce proceedings included an extensive family evaluation by a court-appointed psychologist. This ten-month-long process included interviews, observations, psychological testing, and interactions with me, Susie, and our children. The psychologist also sought out detailed information and accounts of our family engagement from friends, acquaintances, teachers and school personnel, and community members who knew us. This psychologist spent, quite literally, hundreds of hours researching facts and stories about our relationships, and spending time observing us in various family configurations (mother/child, father/child, and each of the children individually). She reviewed reams of documents, including statements from witnesses, police reports, medical personnel in attendance at ER visits, et cetera. Her final report was thirty-eight pages long. In her summary, she recommended that I be granted full custody of the children and that Susie be granted supervised visitation rights. I felt a great sense of relief. This was all I had hoped for: to be able to continue to raise my children in a loving environment.

But the report was not accepted by Susie's counsel and the guardian. I was stunned and appalled. I could not understand how they could ignore the almost year-long assessment and final recommendations of a person who had become intimate with almost every facet of our family relations.

In the spring of 2001—exactly one year after the divorce process had begun—the stress of dealing with Susie's myriad false accusations over such an extended period became too much to handle. I had a physical breakdown. I first had a severe and prolonged attack of Bell's palsy that paralyzed half of my face. I suffered from Bell's palsy for the next two years, with altered speech, impacts on my ability to eat and drink, and an inability to blink or close my right eye for that entire time. Two weeks after the onset of the Bell's, I had a debilitating attack of vertigo that put me in the hospital for several days. I had started vomiting the night before and thought I had food poisoning or the flu. But as the hours passed, the nausea greatly worsened. The room was totally spinning out of control. My friends came over to carry me to the van and drive me to the emergency room. It was a terrifying feeling and I tried hard not to panic. I ended up being admitted to the hospital where I stayed for the next six days hooked up to IV fluids. I remained curled up in the fetal position, unable to move without my world spinning. This was followed by five months of physical therapy to learn how to walk again. I had also lost so much weight that I was very weak. I had to continue working as the expense of the divorce was depleting my funds; I would work for a few hours and then, literally, crawl up the stairs at the clinic to my office where I would nap on the couch.

In the interest of keeping my vet practice going—and dealing with the extraordinary stress of the divorce while still caring for my children's needs—I had totally neglected my own physical and emotional health. My sole driving force had been to gain custody of my children. Susie stated that now with my illnesses, I was unable to take care of my children. It seemed like all of my worlds were spinning out of control; my inside world mirrored my outside world. It would take years for my physical strength, coordination, and balance to fully return.

The lawyer that Susie first hired to handle her end of the divorce decided to quit. The second lawyer that Susie hired recommended that we try mediation. I felt that our interests were just too disparate for mediation to be fruitful. My lawyer felt we had nothing to lose, so we agreed.

On the morning of October 17, 2001, we went to the courthouse for our mediation. After negotiations that took the entire day, we were able to agree on a custody and financial settlement. We would share custody of two of our children and the other four were put exclusively into my care. Susie was granted all of our savings, retirement, the new house and farm, child support, and monthly maintenance. I had to borrow a hundred thousand dollars against the clinic to give to Susie. I was left with no money, but I retained my business. I was completely shocked that we had come to an agreement via the mediation. It was not all I had hoped, as I wanted full custody of all the children, but that proved difficult as the father. I was not worried about the monetary settlement. My children and I had suffered a year and a half of a very brutal divorce. I would take this settlement in order to end the agony.

The following Saturday, I went out with a realtor friend and found a house that fit the needs of my large family. I was moving forward with my life as a single father whose primary duty was now to raise all of my children in the best way possible.

9

LIFE AS A SINGLE FATHER

Immediately after my divorce was finalized and I had purchased the house in which I would raise my children, I turned my energies to my new life as a single father. I had to figure out the logistics of getting my children to and from school, as well as their care after school until I was off work. I had to furnish each of their bedrooms and get some basic furniture for our home. I had to move everything I ended up with in the divorce off the farm. In addition to all this, I was working full-time. I could not afford to take any time off work as the divorce had wiped me out financially.

The most important job of my life has been raising my children; now I'd be doing it as a single man. All of my children had suffered to varying degrees during the divorce. But they had also endured hardship during our marriage, especially the last few years when our arguments were louder and more frequent. My children needed a home where they could heal and grow. I dedicated my energies to providing a loving, stable, and structured place for them where they would once again feel safe.

Bo lived with me full-time and never visited Susie; that was her choice and I respected it. Noel and Mariah spent one week with me and then one week with Susie. This schedule was equitable in terms of the amount of time my girls had with their mother, but it was difficult and unsettling for them to move back and forth so much. Susie and I ran our homes very differently, as I had set bedtimes and normal rules to guide us. Isaiah spent all of his time with me, except every other weekend, when all three of the younger children were at Susie's. Cody was living in Bellingham in an apartment I rented for him while he finished school. I visited him on a regular basis and he came down often to spend time with his siblings. I stayed active in his school activities. Kelly was living in California with her uncle and aunt.

Fortunately, I had a client and a good friend who ran a daycare where Isaiah could go after school. He could ride a bus to her neighborhood and she would walk over and pick him up. She was a very loving person and I knew my son was safe and well-cared for with her. They understood my schedule and would feed him dinner and start his homework on the nights I was at work late. I would have one of my receptionists drive up to Noel and Mariah's school to pick them up on the weeks I cared for them. They would often come to the clinic and do their homework or play upstairs in my office, or go home if their older sister was there.

One Thursday evening the week before Thanksgiving, Bo and I were upstairs watching television when the phone rang. It was Susie. I couldn't believe it. She and I had not spoken for months; we did not even speak or see each other after the arbitration the day our divorce was settled. She wanted some advice on her finances, as she now had to manage her own money. I talked to her for ten minutes and tried to give her sound advice. Susie acted like nothing had happened between us and I certainly did not feel like talking about the divorce. When I hung up, Bo and I just looked at each other in shock; neither of us knew what to say.

Within fifteen minutes, the phone rang again. This time it was my daughter Kelly calling from California. I was surprised that she was calling me; we had been estranged for over a year. She had been the child most caught in the middle of the divorce. Our conversation was tentative at first, as neither of us knew what emotions the other was feeling. When she said she missed me, I wanted to cry. One of the hardest parts of the divorce had been the loss of my relationship with Kelly. I told her I missed her too and that I loved her. I realized what courage it took for

Kelly to call me. That call was the start of our healing as a father and daughter and for our family. Bo and I were both so happy that Kelly had reached out. That night I felt the first glimmer of hope that my life as a single father would work out.

The children were with me for Thanksgiving that first year, but I was in no way ready to prepare a Thanksgiving feast. Fortunately, some very close friends invited us over to their home to share our first Thanksgiving with them. They have known my children since they were young and are more like family than friends. It was a wonderful Thanksgiving meal and we filled their home with our noisy, happy family. I truly felt I had much for which to be thankful.

Early in December, that year I started preparing our new home for the Christmas holidays. Arlington Hardware offers shoppers twenty percent off on the first Saturday of every month, so I went down to buy some decorations. I saw a display of miniature holiday houses that light up. As a child, I was always mesmerized by these little houses and villages I would see in shop windows and at friends' homes. I selected a church with a steeple, a toy store, and two houses, along with a blanket of "snow." They were the start of what my children have come to call my "obsession," as I have continued to collect them throughout the years, moving into the more intricate houses, and setting up entire villages every Christmas. I now have over fifty houses. Secretly, I think my children love them as much as I do; as early as November every year, they ask me if I am going to put out all of my houses for the holidays. Sometimes we would turn off the overhead lights and sit quietly listening to Christmas music in the glow of the lit villages. I also often did this alone after the house quieted down and the children were all in bed.

Those first few months were difficult for all of us as we adapted to a new house and new schedules. Over time, we started functioning as a family. I would wake up early, fix breakfast for the children and pack their lunches. Bo was in high school and would drive herself to school. Isaiah's school bus came early, so I would get him to the bus stop and see him off. Then I'd pick up Noel and Mariah at home and drive them up to their school twenty miles away. I would just make it to work by nine when we opened. On Wednesdays, my day off, I would stay up at the girls' school and do recess duty. Even on the Wednesdays I did not have the girls, I went up to do recess duty so I could see them. After work I would get home and cook dinner. I really worked hard to feed them home-cooked meals, but occasionally I would pick up dinner, such as Chinese food from their favorite restaurant. After dinner we would all help clean up, then do homework. If there was time, we would relax with a board game or television. I set strict bedtimes for them, both to ensure they got enough sleep, but also because I would be exhausted by then and needed some time to relax.

Through the first half of 2002, Kelly and I continued to talk on the phone and also started writing letters to each other. In April she asked if she could move back home and live with me. I was very excited. I had missed her so much over the last two years. We decided she would return home after she finished the school year. I purchased an airline ticket for her in June and Bo and I met her at the airport. We were all really happy to see one another. That weekend, I had a big welcome-home barbecue with all six children. My four-bedroom home was now filled to the brim with five children. There was a nice office that served as Isaiah's bedroom and I fixed up a private area in the big playroom for Kelly. I loved having all the children home.

Being a parent is hard work; being a single parent is even harder. It would be nice to say it was all clear sailing raising all these children. However, with three teenagers and two pre-teenage adolescents, there were many times when situations arose that were difficult for us. I had no one to talk to about how to best handle these problems. But I did my utmost.

Time went on and the changed life all of us were living became the new normal. Cody graduated from high school in 2002 and entered the working world. Bo and Kelly had summer jobs. The three youngest children continued their same schedules, except for two full weeks during the summer that they would stay with Susie. This was a break for all of us and I would take these two weeks to travel.

Bo graduated in 2003 and continued to live with me for two more years as she went to college. I was glad she stayed. She was helpful with her siblings, but mostly I enjoyed her company. Going back and forth was hard on Noel with all of her high school activities. She had decided to go to high school in Burlington with her friends. It was thirty miles away and she felt isolated on the weeks she was with me. She asked me if she could stay full-time with her mom. I reluctantly agreed; I would miss her. She started staying with Susie at the beginning of the school year. She had developed an interest in golf and played on the high school team, so we still spent lots of time together golfing. Over the Christmas holiday that year, after we had celebrated Christmas with everyone, she and I traveled to Myrtle Beach and attended a short golf school together. It was a great trip.

I worked hard to expose my children to various activities. Along with golf, I took my children skiing at Mount Baker and enrolled them in lessons. They enjoyed skiing, but soon transitioned to snowboarding. We also hiked and took trips, both locally as well as back to Colorado for family reunions, when we would travel through Montana and visit Yellowstone National Park. I taught my girls to cook. I purchased a sewing machine and took sewing lessons up in Mount Vernon, so I could teach them the basics. We made pillows and doll clothes. I would take my girls clothes shopping, including to get their homecoming and prom dresses. The first thing I would do when we entered the store was to locate a young, well-dressed saleswoman and let her advise my daughters on fashion. At these times, my responsibility was simply to approve and pay.

One afternoon in the early spring of 2005 when I was out on farm calls, Noel called me crying. She was having difficulty living at Susie's house and wanted to move back. I made arrangements that week for her to move back in with me. We enrolled her into Arlington High School, where she finished her junior year. She really wanted to graduate from Burlington with her friends. She wondered if she could live with someone up in Burlington. She had discussed it with her friend's mom, who was looking for a home to rent after her divorce. I happened upon a house for sale on the golf course that was perfect; it was a two-story home with a downstairs that was set up as a separate living area. I purchased the home and rented the upstairs to her friend and her mom, whom I had known for years and trusted to watch over Noel as she would her own daughter. Noel finished her senior year in this house and I would see her frequently. We would meet for a round of golf or dinner, and she frequently came down to my house to visit. I even caddied for her in a couple of golf tournaments she entered.

In 2005 Kelly graduated, and the following year she joined the army. She went to boot camp in Fort Jackson in South Carolina. I flew down and attended her graduation. I was so proud of her and how much she had grown up. She took advanced individual training for 88M—a motor transport operator—in Fort Leonard Wood in Missouri. She then served two tours in Iraq, totaling twenty-seven months. We all worried about her every day, and I said a prayer for her daily. I was so relieved when she returned from her second tour unharmed physically, although that experience was very emotionally taxing. She was honorably discharged in 2012 as a sergeant.

One Wednesday morning, I was at Mariah's school doing early morning parking lot duty during a week when she was staying with her mom. Susie drove her up and dropped her off. Mariah was crying; this was not something my eighth-grade daughter usually did. I asked her what was wrong, and she said it was hard living at her mom's. I walked over to Susie's car and told her Mariah would not be returning to her home to live. Surprisingly, Susie agreed and from that day on Mariah lived with me except for every other weekend and two weeks a summer.

In time, all of the major celebrations were held at my home. These family gatherings brought us all together in love and laughter. My house was better able to hold us all. Susie was initially invited for many of these feasts. On Thanksgiving, I loved to cook the turkey all day on my Traeger smoker. As it cooked, I would prepare the many accompanying dishes with the help of my children. One of the high points of the day was when I would bring the turkey through the sliding glass doors from my back porch into the kitchen and see everyone's faces light up at the sight of the perfectly browned bird.

Christmas was another time to celebrate family. There are two Christmases that particularly stand out as being special.

The first one was in 2008. I had everyone over for a big dinner Christmas Day. By then, my children ranged in age from twelve to twenty-five years old. Cody had his girlfriend and a couple other friends over, and the girls each had their boyfriends over. It was a full house. The snow started falling early Christmas morning and continued heavily all day. By the time it came for people to leave after dinner, the roads were impassable. Everyone had to stay at my house. Fortunately, we were well-stocked with food. We all started playing outside in the deep snow. I don't remember who came up with the idea to make a giant snow pile—it just seemed like a good idea. I got on my John Deere tractor with a front-end loader and headlights and started scooping up snow from my pasture and piling it on top of my largest woodpile. The kids moved and packed the snow. After an hour, we had a snow hill twenty feet tall, twenty feet wide, and forty feet long. We cut in steps and made three ski "runs" of various difficulty. We played out there all night. By early the next morning, we were totally worn out. We went inside and cooked a full breakfast for whomever was still awake.

The second very special Christmas came in 2009. A few months before the holiday, I had been in deep thought about my children. I considered how quickly they were growing up. Like all children, they each faced particular struggles. I wanted to give them a gift to help them on their life journey, to offer them a little direction. The idea came to me that I would give each of them a word for Christmas; this word would help them focus on an area of their life where I saw they needed help. I contemplated and chose a word especially for each child. I went on a search for a card that contained that word. That Christmas—after all of Santa's presents had been opened—I gathered my children into the living room. First, I read the poem "If" by Rudyard Kipling, as I often did at Christmas. Then I gave each of them their word and read their card aloud to the family. I started with Cody whose word was "purpose." Then Bo received her word: "patience." Kelly's word was "peace," and Noel's was "persistence." Mariah received the word "balance," and Isaiah's word was "responsibility." Each child would come up and we hugged as I handed them their card. It was an emotional experience for all of us. Each of my children talked to me about their word throughout the rest of the day. They still remember their individual word and will, on occasion, mention it. It was my heartfelt gift to them.

During this time, I started dating Kathie, a friend whose horses and dogs I had cared for over the years. We developed a relationship that involved spending time together during the evenings or weekends when my children were with their mother. I enjoyed my time with Kathie and found it a welcome reprieve from the pressures of single parenting. We would frequent bars where we could dance and I would drink. Over time, our relationship evolved to the next stage, which involved a fair amount of travel: motorcycle trips, veterinary meetings out of state, family vacations, romantic getaways, and holidays with families. I enjoyed our time together very much. Yet, right from the beginning of our relationship, I specifically told Kathie that I was not interested in getting married, or adding a stepmother into the mix of raising my children. After all that I had endured in my marriage, I was not emotionally ready to fall in love again nor was I prepared to make a long-term commitment. We had an understanding, then, that marriage was not on the table.

Often when I would go out with Kathie and her adult children I felt free to drink as I wanted. It was easy to justify drinking, and drinking *heavily*, during these times because I wasn't on duty as a parent. I had earned the right to enjoy myself, and "enjoyment" in regard to alcohol often meant indulging to excess. On these occasions when I would get drunk, I became loud, obnoxious, and full of myself. My jokes and stories became larger than life and took over whatever else was going on. Sometimes I would drink beyond this: to a blackout state. Fortunately, Kathie drank very little and was willing to put up with my stupidity, driving me home and caring for me. Other than these child-free times when I felt entitled to drink, I did not drink at home.

My relationship with Kathie slowly deteriorated over time. My unwillingness to commit more deeply and her desire for a greater connection led us to a turning point. I felt it was unfair to continue with our relationship when I knew she needed more than I could offer to her. It was a very sad breakup as we had shared many years of family time and vacations together. After the initial pain of splitting up, we realized we both respected each other. We have maintained a close friendship to this day.

My children continued to grow into adults and slowly leave home. As each one would leave, our home would get a little quieter and seem a little more deserted. In 2011, Mariah graduated from Arlington High School. She stayed two more years as she went to college. It was during this time she developed a passion for glassblowing and moved up to Bellingham to do an apprenticeship. She was fully moved out on her own by mid-2013. Isaiah was close behind, finishing school and gone by the end of that year. I found myself alone, going from being a single father to a single man. It was lonely when I would come home to a house where the only one to greet me was my devoted little dog, Gidget.

Most of my children live close by now and I see them almost daily. I have been blessed with five grandchildren. Not so long ago, when all of my children were living at home and I was exhausted from the demands of raising them, I thought I would not get too involved in their families and kids. I felt I had spent enough time and energy with children. Oh, how wrong I was. As soon as I held my first granddaughter, I was once more overcome with a wave of love and wonder. I have been there as soon as each of my grandchildren were born. Now I spend as much time with them as I can, having sleepovers with all of them at "Pop's" house. They make me feel young and fill that spot in my heart that only grandchildren can fill. I love them so much, and they love me back. Now, when our family gets together there is more noise and laughter than ever, with more faces to light up when I bring in the turkey and more hungry stomachs to fill. I have truly been blessed with good relations with my children now as close friends and people I respect. My kids are the best part of me and have become people I am proud to call *my* children.

10

HARLEY

As soon as I made my final alimony payment to my ex-wife, I went up to the Harley Davidson store in Bellingham and purchased the Harley I had been dreaming about for decades. I had owned and ridden motorcycles since I was fifteen and the vision of riding a Harley had remained with me all these years. I chose a sleek, black Heritage Softail Classic.

That summer of 2004, I rode as often as time permitted, after work and on weekends. When I'm riding, I am present in the moment. The countryside, the feel of the air passing by, the classic roar of the Harley engine, the vibration of the bike, and the attention to the ride keep me grounded in the immediacy of the moment. I don't worry about the past or the future; I'm just there, on the bike traveling down the road. Where the road leads is less important than enjoying the ride. I feel a part of something bigger, like I'm actually part of the world.

The next August, I rode to the big rally in Sturgis, South Dakota for the first time. I loved the ride there. Out on the road I wasn't a veterinarian, nor a craftsman; I was neither rich nor poor. I was simply a rider. My trips to Sturgis were not just there and back. They became times to explore the western states. I rarely made reservations and I had no set agendas. Some days I would get caught up in the back roads, just meandering, and stopping to sit by a stream or gaze up at a mountainside. These were days Mother Nature beckoned me to soak in her beauty. It's odd how relaxed I would become, almost trance-like. Perhaps this is my meditation, the method for me to enter my zen state.

Andy was born in Dublin and is one of the riders I'd met in Sturgis. We discussed the idea of riding Harleys around Ireland. He would be my guide. I was very excited. Ireland had been a place I longed to visit as my family roots begin in County Wicklow. Two weeks prior to my trip, Andy had a crisis and was unable to travel with me to Ireland. I would go on the trip across Ireland on my own. In August 2010, I landed in London and spent three days at Andy's flat overlooking the River Thames. Andy accompanied me across the English countryside in its typical drizzly, overcast weather. After Andy returned home, I headed out across Wales. I went to Holyhead in the northwest tip of Wales and boarded the ferry that sailed across the Irish Sea to Dublin.

I disembarked in Ireland: land of my grandfather, a place he left at fourteen to escape the poverty imposed on his people after centuries of English tyranny. Dublin, the heart of Ireland, was a place I also desired to explore. For three days, I looked into the nooks and crannies of Dublin by bus and by foot. Everywhere I went was a step into Irish history. I spent a very somber time in Kilmainham Gaol, the harsh prison where—after the Easter Uprising in 1916 for Irish independence from England—the English General Maxwell ordered fifteen Irish heroes to be summarily and brutally executed. It was a grim reminder of man's often inhumane treatment of others. Kilmainham is a cold and foreboding structure, made even more sinister by the atrocities that were carried out within its stone walls. It sent a wave of terror down my spine. To be imprisoned in such a place would be terrifying.

The morning came for me to leave Dublin. As if by design, the weather cleared. I was to be blessed with the Irish sun for most of my motorcycle travels across Ireland. Through the lush green rolling landscape, the kilometers ticked by. With each kilometer, I was overcome with a sensation I had never felt before: a feeling of coming home, of belonging, in Ireland. I have been to five continents and never before experienced this feeling. It was truly peaceful. I passed castle ruins and signs announcing names of places that exuded the wonder and romance, the magical, mystical, long-gone ancient Ireland. Places like Kinnegad, Tyrrellspass, Kilbeggan, Ballinasloe, Galway, or Maam Cross, Ballyconneely, Rusheennamanagh, Kylemore, Claddaghduff.

The land changed, especially as I entered the Connemara area in County Galway. Perched on the western edge of Ireland, Connemara is as beautiful as it is rugged. Its beauty is unspoiled, conjuring up images of Ireland long since passed. I traveled its rough, narrow roads to the Boatsman Cottage by the village of Carna, where my good friends from Arlington, Gerard and Amanda, now live. He had been my family doctor for years, having delivered my daughter Noel and caring for all of my children through numerous emergencies. His wife is a wonderful and kind person. Gerard and I rode our motorcycles along the narrow, curvy roads through the Twelve Bens mountains and around the countryside. I spent three days with them, including my fifty-fifth birthday.

In Ireland, the roads have no shoulder. They are bordered on each side by either rock fences or precipitous drops down to the ocean. It's as if Ireland is so small and the land so valuable, they only begrudgingly give space to the roads. On my birthday, I went on a solitary ride on the narrow roads of Connemara, taking a memorable ride up the Sky Road. The Sky Road is made for a motorcycle. Sweeping corners, occasional straightaways, and breathtaking views. At the top, there is a wide view of the Atlantic Ocean. It feels like the edge of the world. It is both stunningly rugged and amazingly beautiful. The next land mass to the west is the United States. I sent my children a picture via text message and wrote, "I think I am as close to heaven as a person can be on Earth."

For ten more days, I continued to explore western Ireland: Galway, the Cliffs of Moher, the Dingle Peninsula, and down to the Ring of Kerry. If Dublin were the heart of Ireland, Galway would be the soul. It seemed each place was more amazing than the last. I could scarcely travel a mile without seeing a place to stop and marvel. Days found me traveling new roads and nights found me in pubs listening to local music and enjoying Irish stout. One of my most memorable nights was in the town of Dingle. There, music is sacred. At one of the pubs bordering Dingle Bay, there was a gathering of local musicians playing. They stopped and gave the microphone to an older man in the pub. *A cappella*, he sang a plaintive Irish ballad in a rich baritone voice that spoke of love lost and suffering. It resonated with me on a visceral level. It was enthralling. I was in love with the land, her people, and her rich and storied history.

I spent the last four days traveling back to the eastern side of Ireland. I visited Arklow, County Wicklow: the land of my grandfather and people. I visited the Catholic church where my grandfather was baptized. It was a profound experience to kneel and pray in the same small church he and his family had attended over one hundred and thirty years ago. Perhaps I was even in the same pew in which my forebears had prayed. I obtained a copy of my grandfather's birth certificate. I needed this to obtain my Irish citizenship, which I did when I returned home. From Arklow, I rode into the Wicklow Mountains. There, nestled in the Valley of Two Lakes is Glendalough, one of the most amazing monastic sites in Ireland, or perhaps in all the world. With its perfectly preserved Round Tower that rises thirty meters above the ruins of what was once a large and bustling monastery, it is an awe-inspiring site. It was one of the centers of knowledge that helped preserve Western civilization through the Dark Ages. The site dates back to the sixth century, when St. Kevin founded the monastery. Most of the churches and buildings were built in the ninth to eleventh centuries. This land, this place, is sacred.

I spent the day at Glendalough wandering the ruins and the ancient graveyards. I appreciated the tombstones adorned with Celtic designs and topped with the classic Irish cross; it is a symbol derived from the Catholic crucifix and the ancient Celtic knot. I found numerous graves of my clans, Kavanagh and Byrnes. This was the actual countryside from which I originated; it gave me a feeling of connection with this Earth and this sacred area. It was a solemn, peaceful grace that imbued my spirit at that moment.

I knew I would return to Ireland. I was tired and content; my adventure had been more than I could have imagined. That night, dreams visited me, carrying scenes of oceans, hills, and narrow roads leading to heaven. All of this was accompanied by somber Irish ballads sung by a stately old Irish man in his deep baritone voice. Ballads of famines, wars, lost lives, and the leaving of Ireland's children. His songs each ended with hope for the future and love of God, man, and Ireland. I had the deep, restful sleep of a soul who has been on a journey—a quest. I had found the peace of my Grandfather's Ireland while traveling the countryside by motorcycle.

11

Mount Kilimanjaro

I sat in the sixteen-thousand-five-hundred-foot base camp of Mount Kilimanjaro at midnight in March 2012. I left my tent—the only one occupying the large campsite—and readied myself for the arduous trek up the tallest mountain in Africa. The night was frigid and dark, a reflection of the immense sorrow I was carrying with me. I had just found out that my oldest brother Jim had died. Before I'd left for Africa, he was in the hospital for routine treatment; he had been battling cancer for thirteen years and hospitalizations were not unusual. Before leaving home, I had called my brother, but he was unable to talk. I asked his wife Cher to tell him that I loved him and would call when I returned.

I had traveled to the amazing continent of Africa with a close friend and his son. We spent three days trekking through nature preserves and observing wildlife. On the fourth day in Africa, we met up with the climbing party and set off on our trek. There were several dozen people also on the mountain, ready to make the climb. The camps were a flurry of activity between the hikers and the support staff of guides, packers, and cooks. There was a palpable excitement in the air, mixed with apprehension about the daunting climb before us.

But short messages started reaching me the first evening of our trek. My brother was much sicker than they originally thought. I was filled with dread. Midmorning on the second day, one of the guides pulled me and my friend aside. An immense foreboding came over me. I knew what was about to come, but I refused to allow the thought to materialize. I don't remember the guide's exact words as he told me Jim had died. My mind was swirling, numb, screaming in disbelief and horror. I felt my body weaken and my knees buckled underneath me. The guide arrested my fall and sat me down on a large boulder. I cried desperate tears. My idol and my rock could not die. The one man in the world I truly admired. The one man who understood me and could quiet my soul. The one man I had always turned to for guidance and wisdom.

I cried. Then I cried some more. The group moved on and my friend stayed back with me. When my tears subsided, I was faced with one decision: to attempt to summit Kilimanjaro or to return home to my family. I had to decide within a day, after which I could not turn back and would be out of cell range. I exchanged texts with family members to seek their counsel. Each one told me to continue. My brother's wife said, "Go on. Your brother would want you to. He would be mad if you quit now." I knew she was right. My brother, Mike, also sent a text and he was even more succinct; he told me to make the climb. I heard and felt their message to me.

I was in a total daze, oblivious to everything except my pain. I followed many paces behind our group, unable to talk or receive their condolences without breaking down. It had been somewhat physically taxing as we trekked on at fourteen thousand feet. Now it was all but impossible. My broken heart was constricted in my chest so tightly that it seemed incapable of pumping blood. My shattered mind could scarcely command my legs to move forward in feeble steps. My breath seemed to come in painful gasps that barely met my needs for life. But on I trudged, realizing I had to decide by the next sunrise.

Sleep did not come for me that night. The frigid air penetrated through me. There was not an area of my body or soul that felt comfort. Lying there engulfed in sadness all alone in my small tent, I decided I would climb on in honor of my brother. I would carry his memory and his love to the summit with me. He had fought his fight, lived a noble life, and now his journey was done. Never once did I hear him complain. This would be our final trip. This would be our legacy together. He was my oldest brother and confidante. He would travel with me up the slopes of Mount Kilimanjaro.

I decided to forgo the extra day of acclimation at fifteen thousand feet. I left the group and traveled on with the guide and an assistant, Barnabas. I was told my chances of summiting would be significantly less without a day to allow my body to adjust to the oxygen deprivation of the ascent. I realized this, but knew I had to move on. Where before forty tents dotted the evening campsite, now there was only mine. My guide and assistant did not camp by me. I found myself truly alone under the infinite expanse of the African night sky. The stars emitted a brilliance that is indescribable at fifteen thousand feet. There was no light from any human source to interfere with their beauty. It seemed I was among the stars, not below them. Each night I cried sobbing tears that literally froze to my face, and each day I cried silent tears as I moved forward on my journey. Jim—my brother, my friend—never strayed from my saddened mind and crushed heart. My guide, assistant, and I walked across a barren landscape as we neared the great mountain. There was nothing growing at this altitude. I trudged across this lifeless terrain, feeling its barrenness inside of me as well.

After two days, we arrived at the base camp at sixteen thousand feet. It was freezing and I was emotionally incapable of sleep, so I lay there in my tent waiting for eleven at night, the time when my guide and I would start the ascent. I was already completely exhausted emotionally and physically, yet I knew I had to press on. This was no longer a physical adventure; it was a spiritual crusade to honor one of my life's chief players. My guide and I started up that steep slope by the light of our two headlamps. We would be the only two people ascending the route that night. I counted the time by steps, by breaths, and by the slow progress made.

With each step I said my brother's name: "Jim." As I felt my strength wane, I would repeat a verse from "If," by Rudyard Kipling:

If you can force your heart and nerve and sinew
To serve your turn long after they are gone,
And so hold on when there is nothing in you
Except the Will which says to them: 'Hold on!'

My brother's name and Kipling's poem served as my mantras to keep me moving. I felt my whole body weaken as I inched closer to the crest of the mountain. The night was eerily dark. The true light of the night came from the stars, points of light so bright there seemed to be a life force within each of them. Perhaps my brother's spirit shone down on me from one of those stars.

At about three in the morning at somewhere around eighteen thousand five hundred feet, the moon rose over the plains of the Serengeti. From such a height, I gazed down upon the moon as it slowly cleared the flat, never-ending horizon below me. It was a full moon and it occupied the entire east sky. Its orbit moved it at a faster pace than I was able to maintain, and soon the moon was level with me. It loomed so large and appeared so close, I imagined I could reach out and touch it. The moon followed my path for a short time and then it proceeded on ahead of me into heights I could only imagine.

On I trudged, my legs aching and screaming to stop. My breath was rapid and shallow, trying to get enough oxygen to feed my body as I struggled upward. My chest ached. My short breaths turned to vapor in the frigid air and froze in my nose and on my skin. I don't know which area of my body resonated with the most pain. My legs, my lungs, or my heart. You cannot carry tears up the slopes of Mount Kilimanjaro, but you can carry a heart full of sadness. Stopping this painful climb crossed my mind, but I would not entertain this thought for very long. I pushed on for my brother. This was *our* journey.

We finally reached the rim of the enormous volcano just as the dark of the night was being replaced by the hint of first light. I felt relief come over me as I reached the crater rim. The summit was halfway around the crater, another four hundred feet in elevation. I had to draw on strength I had long since used up and to call up willpower I no longer had.

I could hardly breathe. Each breath was a loud and laborious gasp. I tried to drink some water to hydrate myself, but I found my water bottles frozen solid. At long last, the summit was near. The wind was howling and there wasn't a part of my body that wasn't numb from cold and exhaustion. Just steps away from the summit, I turned and saw the sun rise over the plains of Africa. I felt Jim's presence with me, by my side, trying to comfort me in my grief. I paused a moment to take in this incredible scene and tell him we made it and that I loved him. I told him that he would always be in my heart. I missed him so much at that moment. I turned and took the final steps up to the very summit of Mount Kilimanjaro. I looked down from the peak and it seemed the entirety of Africa lay at my feet. I picked up four small volcanic pebbles from the apex of the mountain. I placed them in the small plastic container in which I had carried a green glass shamrock given to me by Kathie.

I knew my time at the summit had come to an end. I started my descent.

One foot at a time, I slid down the slopes of Mount Kilimanjaro on loose rocky scree. My thighs screamed in pain, seizing up so severely that I could barely keep myself upright and moving. My feet were pushed forward in my boots and I formed blisters on the top of each toe. I was totally unable to breathe. I arrived back at base camp shortly before noon. With no time to rest, I set off with Barnabas. If I didn't leave right then, I would miss my plane to Omaha where I planned to meet my family for my brother's funeral. I have no recollection of the twenty hours of flights to Nebraska. The lactic acid in my quads had accumulated to such an extent that I could only walk in a rigid shuffle. This was nothing compared to the pain in my heart.

I landed in Omaha on St. Patrick's Day, the day of my brother's funeral. I felt that was a fitting day to send a red-headed Irishman into heaven. After a few flight delays, I arrived an hour after my brother's funeral had ended. Family had gathered at my brother's house for the wake. When I arrived, I was warmly and compassionately greeted by friends and family. They could see my physical and emotional agony. Then my dad came up to me. To this day, his greeting is indelibly etched in my mind. He reached out and pinched my ribs, saying, "Getting a little fat, aren't you?" This was all he could say. I shuffled away to seek others who shared my grief and sense of loss.

This was the third family funeral in as many years. Two years before, my brother Paul's wife Christina died suddenly a day after Thanksgiving. The following July, my oldest sister Terry died after battling cancer. Now we were all gathered once more to mourn the passing of a sibling. Family and friends had gathered downstairs. The stairs had become an insurmountable obstacle in my present state, but with assistance I slowly descended and joined the group to reminisce and to toast Jim's well-lived life with so much love in his path. I could see the deepest pain etched on the faces of his wife and three children. Cher is a nurse. If it had not been for the amazing care and guidance she gave him all those years, he never would have lived with cancer as long as he did. She was wonderful to my brother and I am indebted to her. We all cried together, tears that flowed from an inconsolable sadness and pain. I stayed behind after everyone else left. I spent a week with Jim's family, assisting with the immediate tasks of closing out a life. It helped me feel that I eased his passing for his family.

I realized that my role was to travel in Jim's memory to the top of Africa and then care for his family in their greatest hour of need. I will carry my brother with me for the rest of my life as a beacon of love and a good life. March 2012 will forever be the month of a great accomplishment and a great loss.

12

JODI

I had reached a point in my life where I was considering the possibility of marriage. My children had left home. I considered this a major milestone. I was alone. I had not remarried when I was raising my children, as I did not want to overcomplicate their lives. But now I started entertaining the idea that enough time had passed since my divorce that it might be safe to fall in love again.

My first encounter with Jodi was at the hospital auxiliary Festival of Trees fundraiser held at Cascade Valley Hospital in November 2013; she worked at the local hospital where I served as Chairman of the Board. A week later I met up with a friend at a local brewery. He knew Jodi and told me he thought we would get along well; he recommended that I contact her. I was intrigued with the idea. My friend also shared with me the details of her prior relationship. Apparently, Jodi had been with a man for over ten years but didn't know he was married. This former boyfriend, Jim, split his time between his home and family in Montana and his work stints in the Puget Sound area (during which he apparently lived at Jodi's house). My friend told me that Jodi had only found out two months prior that Jim was still married and had two children. My friend finished by telling me how this news had devastated her.

Jodi worked as an orthopedic physician's assistant. I had been having pain in my right knee for several months and was scheduled for surgery. A few weeks after the fundraiser and my conversation with my friend at the brewery, I went in for my pre-op exam; it happened to be

Jodi who did the exam. The first thing she said after introducing herself was that she knew my daughter, and that our children were friends. We made small talk about our children and laughed. Jodi completed her exam. After I left, I noted that it had been easy for us to carry on a conversation. She was very efficient and competent as a PA. I liked how conservatively she dressed. I started thinking about her and perhaps asking her out on a date. I saw Jodi again on the day of my knee surgery during which she prepped me for the procedure.

On December 30, 2013, I had a few drinks with friends after work to celebrate the year's end. Having gotten her number from our mutual friend, I sent Jodi a text saying "hi" and asked her how her holiday had been. She told me she had just returned from a trip to Hawaii with her children. We sent text messages back and forth a few times that evening, and then I asked her if she would like to get together. We agreed to meet up after work at the Buzz Inn Steakhouse on the first Friday of the new year.

We had a few drinks at the steakhouse and talked for several hours. We enjoyed conversing about our kids and work, and were surprised at how quickly we passed the time. We decided to meet again soon. Over the next few weeks, we got together several more times. Then we decided to go for a hike together on a late January Saturday. Jodi drove over to my house that morning and then we took my truck up to Deception Pass State Park. Jodi had chosen this place. We parked on the south side of the bridge and took the trail down to the beach. Our first pictures together as a couple were taken on that beach with the Deception Pass Bridge behind us. I put my arm around her shoulders, and she laid her head on my shoulder. In the photo, Jodi looked as happy as I felt. We hiked back up the hill and walked out to the middle of the bridge. We looked west out onto the vast expanse of the Strait of Juan de Fuca. We held each other's gloved hands as we talked and admired the scene. When we returned home, I gave Jodi a little goodbye kiss when she got into her vehicle. It had been a great day. I felt the excitement of beginning to court someone special.

Our relationship progressed and we met up several times a week. Most weekends we would take in a dinner and movie on Saturday night. Some nights we would have dinner and drinks and talk until eight or nine.

We started talking more deeply about our past relationships and the pain they had brought us. Jodi also told me about her recent relationship with Jim, sharing the same details my friend had told me about in the brewery a few months before. Her ex-boyfriend had a small airplane he kept at the Arlington airport that he would use to fly back and forth between Washington and Montana. Jodi told me that learning about Jim's deception after all those years had been a tremendous blow. Apparently, she had learned about his marriage through an Internet search that her daughter's boyfriend had done. Jodi told me that when she confronted Jim about still being married, he admitted he was. She specifically said that her relationship with Jim was completely over and she would never go back to someone who had cheated on her. In turn, I told Jodi about my painful marriage, especially how humiliated and hurt I had felt when I learned about the affair my ex-wife had carried on during our marriage. I told Jodi that I had even suffered a physical breakdown and ended up in the hospital for nearly a week because of the pain of the divorce. I also said that I did not think I could survive another betrayal like that. Jodi told me she thought my ex-wife was crazy to cheat on me and lose someone as special as I was. I felt safe with Jodi, and understood by her.

We met for dinner on Valentine's Day and exchanged cards. We had dinner and drinks, and talked the evening away. I felt we got along well and were good for each other. We had both felt similar pain and betrayal in our past relationships. We both were at a stage in our lives where we were unattached and could pursue a relationship together. After several hours, I walked her to her car, and we kissed. It was a very nice low-key date.

A week later, our plan was to meet at my house after work for a drink and then go to Anthony's HomePort in Everett for dinner. I had made reservations for seven thirty. She arrived at my house about quarter to six and I poured a drink for both of us in my kitchen. We sipped our drinks and talked about the day's events. After half an hour in my kitchen, we finished our drinks and Jodi asked me to pour each of us a second drink; she said she wanted to go upstairs and relax on the couch. We went upstairs and soon we were kissing. Jodi stood up, took me by my hand, and led me into my bedroom. Needless to say, we did not make our reservations at Anthony's. It was a very pleasant, memorable night. The next morning Jodi sent me a text asking if I wanted to meet for lunch. We talked and joked about the previous evening's events and we held hands across the table. She said she had to leave after lunch in order to be home for her children, but said she would come over the next day. We found ourselves back in my bedroom.

As our time together became more intimate, so did our text messages. One morning I sent a text to her at work and told her how our relationship brought me peace and how well I had slept after being with her the previous night. She wrote back and said she was glad one of us was peaceful and had slept well. Jodi then said she had been awake all night, thinking about me and how having me in her life changed the way she was planning for the future. To know she was thinking of spending her future with me made it easier for me to think of spending my future with her.

We continued to meet a few times a week and would usually end up back at my house at the end of the evening. Occasionally, Jodi would spend the night. But usually she would go back home. There were also weeks when Jodi would need to be home by dinnertime to be with her children and would be unavailable over the weekend. She told me she needed to spend this time caring for her children. I understood and respected her responsibilities for her kids as I was a single parent also.

As our relationship progressed, Jodi told me that because of the pain Jim had caused her, she wanted to keep certain boundaries to protect herself and her children. She told me her home was a "private sanctuary" for her and her children. She was not ready to bring another man to her home or into her family yet. She told me her children's dad had never been part of their lives. Her former boyfriend Jim had filled that void as a father figure, and the kids even called him "Dad." He bought them cars, helped them financially, and even took them on a trip to California without her. It was difficult on them when they learned he was married. She said in time she would heal, and I would be welcome in her home. I understood this and was willing to give her the time and space she needed to heal.

Jodi also said she wanted to keep our relationship a secret—especially at the hospital—as she didn't want people thinking she was receiving special treatment or favors because she was dating the chairman of the board. I told her that did not make sense to me, as I had nothing to do with daily operations of the hospital or granting favors. But she insisted, so mostly I kept our relationship secret. There were a few people I did tell though, as I was happy to be dating Jodi.

On St. Patrick's Day, Jodi and I met up after work for drinks and a light dinner. I gave her a green gift bag containing a Celtic knot necklace, Irish cookbook, bookmark, and some Irish good luck tokens that I had purchased on my trip to Ireland and had wrapped in green tissue paper; She gave me a St. Patrick's Day card. We enjoyed a very nice evening toasting the Irish and our good fortune to be together. Later that night, Jodi sent me a text message from home, thanking me for all the nice gifts. She told me she had never received such a thoughtful, appropriate and color-coordinated gift from a man. Jodi guessed that raising four daughters must have brought out my sensitivity and creativity.

One Saturday in April, Jodi accompanied me to Darrington for a free pet health care clinic for the many residents of that area who had been impacted and stranded by the tragic Oso mudslide that had occurred recently and which had claimed forty-three lives. It had rocked our small community. Jodi was my assistant as I examined and treated the animals. She took the client and patient information, filled syringes for vaccines and injections, and filled prescriptions. We enjoyed working together as a medical team and talked about how we might do so in the future with her assisting me in surgery.

The next Saturday morning, Jodi came over to my house to go on another hike. This was a warm, sunny, glorious spring day: a perfect day to be outside together. Much to my surprise and delight, Jodi said she wanted to go on a motorcycle ride instead of a hike. I was shocked. She had insisted that she would never ride with me, that motorcycles were too dangerous. I had told her I understood and never asked her to ride with me. Therefore, her request to ride that sunny morning came as a total and pleasant surprise. I had most of the riding gear she needed as I often took my daughters on rides with me. I helped her put on leather chaps and she donned her leather coat and a helmet. She was wearing light tennis shoes and she wanted to change into boots. Jodi asked if we could ride over to her house so she could change into her boots. I agreed to her request and off we went on my Heritage Classic. I spent the first few miles helping her adjust to riding on a motorcycle so that she would feel safe. She directed me to her home on Camano Island and I pulled up to her house. She had me wait outside in the cul-de-sac behind her backyard wooden fence while she went in and changed her footwear. This was the first time I had been to her house. She had not taken me before or even told me where she lived. I could see she had a nice home, but she did not invite me in. Jodi came out of her house wearing her boots and climbed onto the back of my Harley. We spent the day riding the back roads through farm country. Jodi absolutely loved riding with me and soon this became our preferred activity together when the weather was good.

I felt optimistic about our relationship, and Jodi often sent text messages upon returning home from our outings together telling me how much she enjoyed our time together. We talked about our growing affection for each other. I was falling in love with Jodi and I told her that.

She told me she was not yet ready to say she loved me, but said she was getting close. I wanted to do something special for Jodi where we could get away for an overnight. I asked if she would consider going to Seattle with me for the weekend. She checked her schedule and told me that she would be available the first weekend of May. We both happened to have that Friday off from work, so it seemed perfect. Once we scheduled the weekend, I started planning. I booked reservations at a very reputable restaurant and hotel in Seattle, along with a couple's massage and a facial for Jodi. She enjoyed every minute of that evening. The next day we walked hand-in-hand through Seattle's famous Pike Place Market, enjoying the sensory delights of the open-air market. We both carried great memories back with us as we drove home at the end of the weekend. She told me she had never been given such special treatment before. I replied that to me she was special, and I felt good treating her well.

During the month of May, Jodi and I got together a few times. We went shopping one Saturday when I bought her an outfit for our upcoming trip to Las Vegas, during which I was going to meet her younger sister and brother-in-law. I purchased tickets for the four of us to go to a Guns N' Roses concert while we were there for the long weekend. When the end of the month rolled around, we took off for our trip. All of us enjoyed the time we spent together in Vegas, and it was nice to start meeting Jodi's family. This was a notable juncture in our relationship as it was our first airplane trip together. This felt like a step deeper into a committed relationship.

After our return from this exciting and intimate trip to Las Vegas, Jodi became sick and I did not see her for two weeks. I offered to come over and help take care of her, but she would not allow me to come over. During this time, she did not respond to my text messages either. This became a frequent pattern in our relationship: non-communication after some of our extended times away. We would have a good time together exploring some new locale, and then she would be totally unavailable to get together with me for a week or more afterward. It was very disconcerting to me. When I brought it up with Jodi, she simply said I was too sensitive and that I needed to relax.

By the early summer, just five months after our first date, Jodi and I were spending many afternoons and nights together, taking motorcycle rides through the farmlands on back roads and going out to nice dinners. On the last weekend of June, we traveled to Leavenworth and spent Saturday night enjoying each other's company and the quaint Bavarian town. We both had a good time, relaxing on a long Sunday walk by the river. On Monday, we met at the Buzz Inn for dinner and drinks. During our meal, Jodi pushed a small white piece of paper across the table to me, smiling and saying, "Now you can start sending flowers to my home." I had been anonymously sending flowers to her at work every few weeks. The paper she had slipped to me during dinner had her home address written on it. I felt her barriers coming down and I thanked her. The next day I sent a bouquet to her home.

But in the middle of July, we had a setback. During a dinner date, Jodi expressed anxiety about her mother's impending visit. Apparently, her house and yard were a mess because we had been spending so much time together and she hadn't had time to do yardwork. Jodi didn't want her mom to see the shape her house and yard were in. At that moment, I knew what to do. I had Friday off from work, so I went over to Jodi's house to clean up the exterior in preparation for her mom's visit. I wanted to surprise her by having it all done before she arrived home from work. I spent my entire day off mowing, weed eating, picking up spilled garbage, and tidying up her front yard. Toward the end of the day, I received a call from Jodi. She seemed tense and asked me what I was doing. I told her I was enjoying the day; I still wanted the yard cleanup to be a nice surprise for her. Jodi questioned me further, asking where I was. Her tone was stern. Finally, I told her I was doing her yardwork as a surprise for her. She sounded very perturbed and questioned me about why I was doing that. When I explained my motivation (to make it nice for her mom's visit), she said "okay" and then asked if I'd seen anyone pull up. I thought this was a strange question, but I hadn't seen anyone and told her this.

When we got together briefly at my place a few hours later, Jodi was still clearly upset about me being at her house and barely thanked me for the cleanup work I'd done. She said she felt I'd invaded her privacy. I apologized, saying that I wouldn't do it again; I was only trying to help her feel less anxious. She left shortly after this conversation. But several days later, the thread of this conversation picked up again in a phone call. Jodi told me that Jim had heard I'd been cleaning up the yard and was upset about it. I told Jodi I thought it was none of Jim's business who was at her house, as he ought to be concerned with his own wife and kids back in Montana.

During her mom's visit, Jodi brought her mother to my house to watch my young grandchildren while I went to a hospital board meeting. Upon my return, I made a nice barbecue meal for all of us. Jodi had told her mom we were just "friends." But later when I asked Jodi what her mom's impression of me was, she told me that her mom thought I was nice and said, "At least he's single." The latter seemed to be a reference to Jodi's former affair with Jim.

Toward the end of July, we went on a weekend motorcycle trip to the Olympic Peninsula and then over to Port Townsend. I bought Jodi a pair of cowgirl boots as we strolled through town. We enjoyed intimate conversations which filled me with hope for a future with Jodi.

I had noticed that Jodi wore a ring on the fourth finger of her left hand and when I asked her about it, she told me it kept away unwanted attention from men. It was a ring Jim had bought for her. I was uncomfortable with her wearing a ring from another man, especially one who had apparently done her such wrong. I asked if she would be comfortable accepting a promise ring from me. Without hesitation, she said she would. A few days later we went to Costco where she picked out a beautiful ring. This felt like another big step forward in our relationship.

The first week in August found me traveling alone to Sturgis for the big motorcycle rally. Jodi and I kept in regular contact via texts and phone calls. We both said we missed each other. While there I bought her some nice Harley shirts and jewelry made from Black Hills gold. I sent several postcards to her home address from Deadwood and Sturgis. We decided that when I got home, we would take a motorcycle trip together over Highway 20 to Winthrop.

That Saturday morning in mid-August was perfect as we headed east over the Cascade Mountains. We stopped at the Diablo Lake Overlook and asked a fellow traveler to take our picture together with the lake in the background. Having Jodi on my bike felt so natural. It felt right being together. We stayed that night in The Bunk House Inn perched on the hill overlooking Winthrop. We cleaned up and walked to the Arrowleaf Bistro for a nice dinner, and then strolled down the street on the wooden sidewalks to the Old Schoolhouse Brewery, where we sat under the star-filled night sky by the river and listened to music. We even danced together for the first time, something Jodi told me she had not done in years. The entire evening felt good.

There are rides that seem perfect: weather, scenery, roads, and—most of all—perfect company. There was nothing more I needed to be truly happy on that Sunday returning home from Winthrop. That sublime feeling of perfection rode with me and Jodi all the way over the Cascades. That night I sent Jodi the picture of us at Diablo Lake. I told her what a great time I had with her. She replied, "Yes. It was. Thank you so much for being such a good person to me and for me. I'm always at peace when I'm with you." That night when I went to bed, I was happy to be with such a wonderful woman. I envisioned more great weekends in our future.

Monday was a workday for both of us. In the early afternoon, a group of Harley riders thundered past my vet clinic. Instantly, I thought of our weekend trip and I sent a text to Jodi to see how her day was going. I received no response. I assumed she was busy. I checked my phone throughout the afternoon and evening but still received no response. The next day I reached out again, and again got no reply. My cycle of anxiety in the face of Jodi's silence began. I sent a message asking if anything was wrong or if I'd done something to offend her. Still, nothing. On Wednesday morning, I sent an angst-filled text wondering if I'd inadvertently hurt her in some way. Finally, though briefly, she replied. Jodi said that I should settle down, things were fine, and she would call me when she got out of the next surgery at work. But she never called. Later that day, I happened to pass her on the street on my way to the hospital for an employee barbecue. She was just leaving. We talked briefly but Jodi seemed nervous and wanted to get home. What struck me was how starkly different this was from how we'd been when we were together just three days prior. It upset me to not know or understand why she was acting so distant and aloof.

Over the next two days, I sent messages checking to see if she wanted to get together for a ride or a drink. I heard nothing back from her. Because it was so sunny and warm on that Friday, I went out for a ride on my motorcycle. I ended up at the Stanwood Saloon. I sent a text message to Jodi, inviting her to come out with me for a ride. She didn't reply. I then began alternating between sending texts and waiting for a response that would never come, and drinking beer after beer. I added to the mix in my system, some whiskey (to "take advantage of the football game drink special"). I became more and more remorseful and anxious. I tried calling Jodi, but she didn't answer. My texts became more pleading and I sank into a deep depression. I begged Jodi to come get me as I knew I had reached a point of no return. I needed her help. No response. I drank until I could drink no more. The bartender took my helmet and motorcycle fob; it was obvious I was far too drunk to ride. I went out to my bike anyway and sat on it. All eight hundred and fifty pounds of it fell over on top of me. I next remember a large Stanwood police officer standing over me and then hoisting my motorcycle off me. The choice he gave me was to go to jail for the night to sober up, or to be taken to the house of any friend who might live nearby. I asked him to take me to Jodi's house. Though she wasn't there, her friend and daughter were. I could barely walk and kept sliding off the couch in her living room. Jodi's friend said I had to leave before Jodi arrived back; her friend drove me home.

The following morning, I was mortified by my actions of the previous evening. I had broken two of Jodi's cardinal rules: getting drunk, and going over to her house. I was terribly hung over with a pounding head and nausea. But the emotional pain was far worse. I wondered how I could have been so stupid. My inability to control my drinking had cost me someone I loved; I knew that it was over with Jodi. I had just lost my last chance at true love because of my insecurity and weakness, as well as my inability to control my alcohol consumption. I was destined to be alone and lonely. I sent a text to Jodi apologizing and begging her forgiveness. I promised to change if she gave me one more chance. I sent another similar text message the next day. This continued for two more days, one of which was my fifty-ninth birthday. She did not respond to a single one of these messages.

On the Wednesday following my drunken night, she finally responded to a text message. She said she could not tolerate that kind of behavior in her life and asked if I wanted to meet so she could talk to me in person. I did. When we met later at the casino, she told me that her father and ex-husband were alcoholics and she could not be with another one. Jodi told me we were through. I asked about our planned trip to Italy for that coming October. She would not go with me. Though she cared for me, she said, she needed me to work on my emotional stability. I asked her about her relationship with Jim; someone had sent me a picture of him kissing her on the cheek in a restaurant the previous week and my daughter-in-law had seen them together at Safeway the day I ended up at her house, drunk. She told me that Jim had asked her for medical advice and she reiterated how much she despised him for deceiving her all those years. We parted ways. After eight months of increasing intimacy and plans for the future, Jodi and I were over.

The next morning, I sent a text message thanking her for her concern for me and asking if I could get my Italy travel guide back from her. A few days later she came to my clinic unannounced and had my book with her. We had a private conversation during which I apologized again for my behavior. I was a wreck. I implored Jodi to tell me what to do, how I could work through this. She told me I needed counseling. This made sense to me. I knew I couldn't continue on my own and I had nowhere to turn for help. I decided that evening that I was in such acute pain, I needed to seek therapy. After a few calls with several different therapists, I found one to be especially kind and understanding. I needed her perspective; intimate relationships with women seemed to be the area of my life in which I had the most dysfunction. This notable therapist, Susan, appeared to offer what I needed. I scheduled our therapy sessions to start just after I returned from my trip to Italy.

After Jodi ended our relationship in August of 2014 because of my drinking, I accepted all blame for my actions and carried around a heavy load of shame. I did not believe I was an alcoholic, but I believed that my drinking had been a justifiable reason for Jodi to leave me. I realized I could not do anything to change what had happened. I knew Jodi and I would never get back together; she had been very clear about that. She gave me no second chance and no room for redemption. I accepted that she was out of my life as far as a romantic relationship was concerned.

A few months later, I saw Jodi at a meeting honoring the hospital employees. She came up to me and we talked for the first time since our breakup. It was nice to speak with her. I felt comfortable enough, even after all we'd been through, that I imagined one day being platonic friends with her. Apparently, she felt that same way; over the next several months we'd run into each other occasionally and we conversed easily.

In late May, nine months after Jodi had ended our relationship, she sent me a text message telling me that she wanted to talk. We met at a new wine bar she liked. She told me she missed me and since I seemed to have changed with my work in therapy, she wanted to start a new relationship with me. Jodi said she had not dated or been with anyone else since our breakup. She wanted to start out slowly and see how our relationship progressed. I only took a day to consider her offer. I decided to re-enter a relationship with her. I had fallen quickly and deeply in love with her during those first eight months together, and I felt our relationship still had potential to become the long-term happy marriage I had always sought. I also wanted to prove to her and to myself that I *had* changed and that I could handle our relationship. I had been going to therapy for more than six months and felt I had made some progress in my life and with my emotions. This second time going into an intimate relationship with Jodi, I was very determined to follow her rules so that it would work. I believed she made these restrictions because of the pain she had suffered in her relationship with Jim; she needed to feel safe. I wanted to respect that pain and give her time to heal. I didn't want to ruin it again with my alcohol or anxiety about her inconsistent communications; these two things had clearly angered her. I became even more dysfunctional in our relationship this second round. I accepted her frequent lack of communication as a normal part of our relationship. I also kept this news of restarting my relationship with Jodi a secret from my therapist and family; I felt sure none of them would support my decision to get back together with Jodi.

Our outings started with daytime or evening motorcycle rides and walks on the Centennial Trail after work. It felt natural to be with her again. Quickly, the former patterns of our relationship re-emerged, and we fell into the routines we had established during our first romance the prior year. Essentially, we picked up where we left off. There would be weeks during which we would get together two or three times, sometimes late into the evenings and on the weekends. Then there were weeks where she was busy and had to be home early; during these weeks she was unavailable during the weekends as well. I didn't question this. Her explanations for the stretches of time during which she couldn't spend time with me always revolved around her work and her children. So, while the rhythm of being with her alternated between frequent contact and hardly any communication—a pattern I found increasingly disconcerting and odd—her reasons for this were understandable to me and I forced myself to accept this pattern.

My Harley once more became our primary recreation. One Saturday, we took the ferry to Kingston and had bike seats custom fit for each of us, along with a special backrest for Jodi. I wanted her to be very comfortable on our long road trips. The next weekend we rode over Highway 20 and things felt very easy with Jodi. We were in a good space together and we considered this one of our favorite motorcycle trips. The weekend provided sunshine, relaxation, and good company. Our relationship was back on track and I once more allowed myself to feel safe enough with Jodi to love her and start envisioning our future together.

As the summer progressed, I brought up the idea of taking a trip to Las Vegas and the Grand Canyon. Jodi was excited at the prospect as she had never seen the Grand Canyon. She gave me the dates that she could go on this trip. I immediately went to work planning our travel itinerary while she made reservations for our meals and a massage. She made several of the reservations under the name "Jodi Cavanagh." She laughed when she told me she had done that. She said that she liked using my last name and that it was good practice. It seemed marriage was on her mind just as it was on mine.

Our trip to Vegas was memorable. We ate at some of the upscale restaurants where Jodi had made reservations and stayed at the Paris Resort on the Strip. We also went to a show. I rented a Harley and we cruised from Vegas to the Grand Canyon, riding along Route 66 as much as we could. We took a helicopter ride over the canyon and I took photos of us in the helicopter wearing our headsets, smiling. It was an epic trip for both of us.

A trip we'd planned for late summer to the Methow Valley was thwarted by a raging fire. I had been excited for this trip because I was going to treat Jodi to horseback riding and a hot air balloon ride there, two activities she had never done but wanted to. At the last minute, we had to change our plans as wildfires were causing severe air quality problems in eastern Washington; instead, we enjoyed a lovely trip to Victoria, B.C. (a place Jodi had been hoping to visit). We did all of the high-class activities that the port town has to offer, including high tea and dinner at the Empress Hotel and a tour of Butchart Gardens. Jodi was appreciative of our trip and emphasized how much she enjoyed being with me. She again told me that I treated her in a more special way than anyone else ever had. I told her I treated her that way because that is how I felt about her.

On the trip back from Seattle after our return from Victoria, we stopped at Lowe's Home Improvement. Jodi's washing machine was starting to fail and I had agreed to loan her money to buy a new one, as she was short of money due to unforeseen expenses with her children. While we shopped, she told me her dryer was starting to have problems too and she wondered if I could loan her enough money for a set. I agreed, lending her about eighteen hundred dollars for a high-end pair. The appliances were delivered to her house the next day.

The first Sunday in October, we went to a chocolate festival at the Seattle Convention Center. We stumbled upon a kitchen and bath show that was simultaneously going on. We went in to look at the various displays. Jodi found the stove that she had been reading about and re-searching. It was a professional-grade stove that she loved. When I saw the price tag, I was shocked; I didn't know that stoves could cost that much. Jodi asked if she could have it when we built our home togeth-er. I told her we could, as I viewed it as a tool and bought high-quality tools for myself.

On another occasion in October, we met for a motorcycle ride up to La Connor. The fall weather was getting cooler and the nights shorter, so this was to be our last ride. As we were leaving, Jodi told me to take the long way up to Pioneer Highway as she wanted to show me something. I did as she asked. Heading north out of Stanwood, we crested a hill where there was a pasture with a beautiful west-facing, panoramic view of the Puget Sound and the San Juan Islands. Jodi pointed at the pasture where about fifteen Jersey heifers were grazing and said, "Just take the cows out; don't you think that would be the perfect spot for our new home?" Looking at the view, I could easily envision our house on the hill and spending my future with Jodi admiring the vista. We both smiled. Again, I had the strong sense that Jodi was considering a lifelong relationship as my wife.

I loved Jodi to no end; it is no overstatement to say that I was head-over-heels in love with her. Because of this, I was eager to provide experiences for us that would make beautiful memories we could look back on. I had always envisioned having a marriage for life and spending time in old age looking back on the memories we'd created. But here I was a sixty-year-old man dating a middle-aged woman and I could feel the tug of time on our relationship. I wanted us to have memories that we could reminisce together about later, as man and wife. I knew we didn't have enough time in our lives to go to each destination repeatedly, so I strived to make every trip as special as possible. I have always been a bit old-fashioned in how I treat women; I love to hold the door for them, give gifts, and behave gentlemanly. Even during times in my life when I had no cash flow, I treated my girlfriends to handmade gifts. I have always been this way. Because I happen to have done well in my passionate work as a veterinarian, it was easy for me to justify the expenses of nice clothes for Jodi, expensive meals at fancy restaurants, exclusive accommodations, and once-in-a-lifetime adventures. I have always treated my sweethearts well and shared everything I have with them, materially and emotionally.

It was totally natural, then, to be this way with Jodi. Our trip to New Orleans (the weekend after a veterinary conference I had attended there all week) in November 2015 was no exception. Her birthday had been on Halloween, but she was out of town for work that day. I had promised her that the New Orleans trip was to celebrate her birthday together. I flew Jodi there for a four-day weekend and followed her lead as she booked reservations for us at the finest establishments Louisiana had to offer. I also treated her to an extravagant birthday gift: a complete outfit (including shoes) that she got to pick out at a boutique store. The day after our return, we met for dinner and I gave Jodi the clothes and shoes I had purchased for her in New Orleans; I had packed them in my bag because the one she'd taken was too small to carry them.

The following two weeks, we did not see each other. Jodi said she was busy at work. Then she became so sick during Thanksgiving week that she couldn't cook Thanksgiving dinner for her kids. I offered to smoke a turkey for them, but she declined. By December, Jodi had recovered from her illness and we met up on several different evenings for dinner or drinks. We were both anticipating our trip together to Seattle before Christmas, where we'd planned a romantic getaway around a Seahawks game.

13

FALLING OFF THE EDGE

Our late-December weekend in Seattle to watch the Seahawks play and to stay in a nice hotel soon arrived. I had also booked a special couple's massage for Saturday. After our treatment, the massage therapist asked me if Jodi was my wife. I said that she was my girlfriend. The therapist replied, "You two make a nice couple." When I later told Jodi about this, she just smiled and said, "We do." On Sunday morning, we explored Pike Place Market and then spent the afternoon at the game. We walked back to the hotel to warm up, shower, and dress for dinner. After an excellent low-key dinner, we retired to our room for the night. Jodi wanted to watch television to relax, so we found a James Bond movie. As we were watching, Jodi sat up in bed with her back to me and was texting on her phone. She had never done this before. When I asked her what she was doing, she replied that she was just checking her email. I found this odd.

I spent the next day in my shop to finish carving the thunderbird I was making as a Christmas present for Jodi; it was just a few days before Christmas. I was making this gift to honor her Native Alaskan heritage and her Thunderbird Clan of the Tlingit tribe. I was excited to give it to her. We communicated via texts on Christmas Day and arranged to meet on the 26th to exchange gifts. I presented her a few nice gifts. Then I told her to close her eyes and I laid the three-piece wood carving on the table and had her open her eyes. She absolutely loved it. Jodi also gave me some lovely and substantial gifts that I took as her showing she cared for me. We were only able to spend two hours together; Jodi had to get back home to her children. We talked about getting together before New Year's Eve for drinks to celebrate the end of 2015 and the start of 2016, a year I thought held great promise for us. Jodi couldn't get together on New Year's Eve, as her son was having friends over and she needed to be home to watch them. She assured me we would meet up in the next few days before the end of 2015.

I sent texts and called Jodi over the next several days. But she mostly didn't respond; when she did text, it was with single-word responses. She had agreed to take me to my early morning dentist appointment on Wednesday. I had an abscessed tooth that needed to be pulled. After my tooth extraction, I walked the two miles to my clinic and had a receptionist drive me home. I sent a text message to Jodi later and told her I was home and not in much pain. She simply texted back, "Good."

On New Year's Eve, I sent several texts to Jodi and tried once to call her to set up a time to meet for a celebratory drink. I received absolutely no response from her. Even for Jodi, this was an abnormal lack of communication. I was starting to feel anxious and wondered why she wasn't answering. I spent that evening celebrating with my daughter, son-in-law, and two grandchildren who were temporarily living at my home. We did not drink alcohol. We played games and celebrated together as a family. An hour and a half before the turn of the New Year, I sent a text to Jodi to wish her "Happy New Year." I wondered how she was faring as she watched over her son and his friends. I hoped she was having fun. Again, I received no response. I kept checking my phone and becoming increasingly anxious. I simply wanted to meet up with the person I cared so deeply about so we could celebrate the new year together. But receiving no response added to my anxiety. I was ramping up. As the countdown to midnight grew near, I continued to repeatedly check my phone, with increasing frequency, to see if she had sent good wishes. My mind started wondering why she hadn't responded to any of my attempts to reach her. It had been nine days since our intimate overnight in Seattle and five days since we had exchanged Christmas gifts. I wondered what had happened and if I had done something wrong. I paid less and less attention to my grandchildren and more and more attention to my phone. I was hoping and praying Jodi would text or call me and relieve my angst. But nothing came in.

Then an ominous feeling came over me that I have only felt once before. It happened the night I found my wife over at her boyfriend's house with one of my daughters. I told myself I was overreacting, that things were fine, and Jodi was just busy with her children. But the anxiety heightened and the voice in my head would not stop. I knew I was being foolish and oversensitive; Jodi always told me that when I was anxious I would too easily spin out of control.

Finally, just thirty minutes before midnight, I decided that the only way to calm my anxiety and quiet the voices was to go over to Jodi's, see that she was home, and then I would be fine. I wouldn't stop and talk with her; she still kept home off limits as her "private sanctuary." I drove over there. She was not home. I realized this because the only lights on in the house were her son's upstairs bedroom lights over the garage. Apparently, only her son and his friends were home. There was no other sign of life in the house. I did not know what to think. I wondered where she was; perhaps she had just run to the store to get snacks for her son and his friends. I had hoped Jodi would be home and then my worries would have been baseless: just my anxiety getting the best of me. But she wasn't there. At that point, my anxiety began to spin out of control. And, I still wanted to believe everything was fine.

I decided to wait for a time to see if she would come back home. At one thirty in the morning, I was ready to leave and head back home. Just as I was starting my truck, a white car pulled into her driveway. I waited a few minutes before walking over to see a white 1999 four-door Buick Park Avenue sedan with Montana license plates. My heart dropped. Her garage door was open and in front of the Buick, parked in the garage, was Jodi's silver Porsche Boxster. My head began to spin. I wasn't sure what this all meant, but I had a sinking feeling. I walked around to the back of the house. I had never done that before. There was nothing I could have done to prepare myself for what I was to see next.

There are seconds—those snippets of time measured by the incremental movement of the thinnest, fastest hand on the time clock—that inextricably and totally change our lives. An event so sudden and profound in its effect on our psyche that we can never go back to the space in our minds and lives we occupied just that second ago. These seconds alter all we know, all we believe, all we hold dear. This was such a second in time for me, that second that altered my life, that second that sent me into one of the darkest times I have ever experienced. What I saw through the delicate white lace curtains was to forever change my life. Crushed in that instant was all hope for my future. Completely extinguished in that moment were my dreams. Shock and shame descended on me in a tidal wave of emotion that left me unable to move or breathe. I could not, at that moment, even in small measure, comprehend what I saw and all that it meant. The scene I witnessed through that frilly curtain would haunt me day and night, and lead me to reckless actions that would put my very welfare in peril. It marked the beginning of the end and the end of the beginning. No moment in my life has defined me, determined my course, more than that instant.

There, through the type of curtains that are used to imbue a room with softness and purity, I saw Jim standing naked in the middle of Jodi's closet.

Through Jodi's bathroom window, through her white lace curtains, I saw Jim. Unclothed. Fully naked. He was neatly hanging up his clothes into a white plastic garment bag. This was the moment, the instant, I felt the world as I knew it collapse. My dreams imploded. My world shrunk to include only Jim, Jodi, and me. I could not fathom what was happening. How could Jodi lie and deceive me as she had? She knew I loved her; I told her so explicitly. She held my heart in her hands and she crushed it. How could she cheat on me? Slowly I realized she wasn't cheating *on* me. She was cheating *with* me. She was cheating on Jim—who was cheating on his wife—with me, except I hadn't known I was the "other man."

The night air temperature was twenty-three degrees Fahrenheit and my breath formed a vapor as I breathed. But I did not perceive the cold as I stood there in shock and disbelief.

Jim then walked through Jodi's bedroom into the kitchen where I could see him through the window; he was still naked as he looked through some mail on the counter. The way Jim walked around Jodi's house showed me he was very comfortable being in her home, that he knew her son's behavior well enough to know that he wouldn't be downstairs while Jim was naked in the kitchen. After several minutes in the kitchen, Jim walked into Jodi's bedroom and climbed into bed next to her and turned off the light.

I was confused as I turned away and walked to my truck. A million thoughts were bouncing around in my head. I began to realize how I had been used. If she cared for me even a little bit, she never would have led this double life of deception. I drove home and got into bed. I cried most of the night and didn't sleep at all. I felt so humiliated and ashamed of being used, of being so foolish.

For the entire week, I could not get the image out of my mind: Jim naked in Jodi's house, getting into bed next to her. I couldn't sleep well. If I did fall asleep, I would dream about it and then wake up in a cold sweat. I didn't eat. I was very, very sad and depressed. I desperately wanted to have an in-person conversation with Jodi. But my attempts to reach her went unanswered.

In the middle of that week, I went to my therapy session with Susan. I had not told her that I'd gotten back together with Jodi eight months ago. I had kept this information from my therapist because I knew Susan didn't think Jodi had been kind to me the first time we'd been together. She had told me that I could not trust Jodi. I had not believed Susan back then. But on this day, though I truly dreaded telling her what I'd kept from her for so many months, I told Susan everything. Now it was painfully clear to me that Susan had been right in her assessment of Jodi's character. I told Susan how Jodi and I had gotten back together and some of the adventures we had enjoyed. I also told Susan how I had seen Jim naked in Jodi's house a few days prior, early in the morning on New Year's, and that they were still apparently together. My mind was a chaotic jumbled wreck and I had trouble focusing on what I was telling Susan, or what she was telling me. I was in the excruciating pain of knowing I'd been used by Jodi.

Susan was shocked about everything I was telling her. Had we not established such a deep bond in our therapeutic relationship over the past year, I suspect my counseling session—and our relationship as therapist/patient—would have ended right then and there. Very fortunately for me, Susan cared enough about me and saw the agonizing emotional pain I was experiencing. Susan really tried to help me that day, but I was beyond help. At the end of our fifty-minute session, I arose from the chair to leave. Just as I opened the door to exit, Susan cautioned me to be careful because I was so distraught. I assured her I wouldn't do anything foolish and I walked out the door.

The next evening, I tried to call Jodi on her home phone. She didn't answer, so I sent a text message to her cell phone. It simply read: "Why? Tell me, Jodi, why?" Within minutes she called me from her home phone. She told me some story about her car still being in the shop since before Christmas (the vehicle I'd seen in her garage just a few nights before) and that she'd been sick. Toward the end of the phone call, I asked, "Jodi, are you seeing someone else?" With an instant and indignant reply, Jodi said she was not and wondered why I would even ask that question. She then went on as she often did about how oversensitive I am and that I overreact, how I need to settle down and chill out. Jodi told me to quit worrying about our relationship, that everything was fine. Before hanging up, she said she'd be in touch with me soon so we could meet up. I said okay, wished her a good night, and hung up. I went through this formality of kindness in the call (as if I believed her; as if everything was fine in our "relationship"; as if I hadn't seen another man naked in her house, in her bedroom, in her bed) because I really wanted to see her in person so I could confront her with what I had seen and now knew.

My first thought upon hanging up was how Jodi lies just like my ex-wife. My second thought was, *Tim, you have a problem.* I realized that I had picked two women to care for and decide to marry who ended up lying to and cheating on me. That was *my* problem.

Confusion, pain, and shame all weighed heavily on me. I had not told anyone except Susan about my betrayal and agony. This was an immense burden to shoulder alone. I felt valueless; I felt less than human. To be treated so cruelly by the woman I loved seemed to indicate I was not worthy of love and respect. The place within me that had held a lifetime of accumulated shame cracked wide open and I was engulfed by it all.

The following night, I went to a retirement party for a longtime employee of the hospital. I repeatedly made toasts to anything I could think of, as I desperately wanted to drink enough to forget—even if for just a short time—how my life had imploded. But I could not drink enough to ease the heartache. The sole thought occupying my drunken mind when I left the dinner party was that I had to catch Jim and Jodi together, so she would be forced to tell me the truth. I had spent seven days in agony, and I felt the only way to find peace was to see her face-to-face and have her witness my pain. I wanted her to apologize. I wanted to be treated as a human being. Driving back to my house that night, I decided to go to Jodi's to see if Jim was there. I went home to get a stocking cap because it was in the low twenties Fahrenheit. In a drawer in my Harley room, I saw the balaclava that I'd purchased in Sturgis for Jodi, to keep her warm during our motorcycle rides. The frigid temperature outside led me to don the face mask. In my drunken logic, it seemed the right choice both for warmth and secrecy—a choice that would come to haunt me later in public opinion and in court. I was still wearing the beautiful maroon dress shirt, decorative black western-style vest, black dress jeans, and a warm black jacket that I had worn to the retirement gala. The "irrational logic" of being at my wit's end, very inebriated, and a week with virtually no sleep led me back to Jodi's house—and back to that fateful window.

On the drive over to Jodi's, all I could think of was her lying to me during all of the time we had spent together. I felt like such a fool to have loved her. When I arrived in her neighborhood, I decided to park in the small graveyard across the street from her house. When I walked across the street to her home, I saw Jim's green Ford truck parked in the same spot his Buick had been the week before. His truck door was unlocked when I tried it. Inside I saw numerous receipts. I went through them quickly and saw some showing that he had been with Jodi the week of Thanksgiving when she had been "too sick" (she said) to get together. I also saw receipts showing that Jim had been in town from Christmas through New Year's, during the period Jodi and I had gotten together and exchanged Christmas presents. I took these so I could show them to Jodi when she lied to me again. I wanted proof of their being together—proof that even Jodi wouldn't be able to refute.

I wandered around to the back of the house where I'd been a week earlier. The lights were off in Jodi's bedroom, so I assumed Jim was in bed with her. I wanted to catch them together and in my inebriated state, I decided that I'd open a window and listen for their voices. I pushed open the very same window through which I'd seen Jim naked just a week before. Just as the cuff of my heavy winter coat caught on the lower left corner of the screen, the lights came on. Jodi burst into her closet wearing an embroidered white linen nightgown and yelled, "What the F - - - !"

Panic set in and I instinctively broke into a run across the street to the graveyard. In that moment, I made the decision to hide in the woods on the edge of the graveyard. I lay down on the wet, icy, frigid forest floor. And I waited. I soon saw police lights at Jodi's house and within minutes there were two sheriff cars on the road in the graveyard, parked on either side of my truck. Shortly after that, the sheriffs were at the edge of the woods calling to me to come out; they threatened to send in the dogs. I lay there drunk, dazed, confused, and panicky. I half walked and half stumbled out into the road. They immediately threw me back onto the frozen ground—belly down—and handcuffed me with my arms behind my back. There were at least four sheriffs surrounding me with their guns drawn. What they saw was a criminal wearing a black ski mask (the gift of a balaclava for Jodi) to hide his face and who was dressed in black. They did not see a middle-aged professional who was drunk and in immense emotional pain.

I was incoherent as I desperately and drunkenly tried to explain my behavior. I wanted them to understand that I wasn't a hardened criminal behaving aberrantly; I was a rejected, betrayed boyfriend seeking the truth. They drove me sixty miles from Camano Island around to Coupeville. During the course of my transport, the liquor I'd consumed at the retirement party started wearing off. The pain of my arms locked behind me as I sat on the hard plastic seat of the squad car brought into focus for me the stark reality of my plight. The last week had seemed like a terrible nightmare. Now I seemed to be in a surreal world where only chaos and pain remained.

After sixty years on Earth, this was my first night in jail. I sat all night on my hard bed, unable to comprehend what had happened to my life. A mere week ago it had held so much promise and hope for the future. Finally, in the afternoon of the next day, I was led out of the jail for a telephone hearing with the Superior Court Judge pertaining to the charges filed against me and my release. The judge recounted the charges and the terms of my release. She told me I could not go within five hundred feet of Jodi or her house. She asked me if I understood; I replied that I did. She then asked the deputy if she had forgotten anything. He replied that she had fully covered the terms of my release. When he released me, he reiterated exactly the same terms of my release as the judge had clearly stated—I could not go within five hundred feet of Jodi or her house. What I would find out a week and a half later is that I was also prohibited by the NCO (No Contact Order) to go onto the hospital property where Jodi worked. This was never stated aloud before I was released, and it only appeared in one of two copies of the written NCOs that I received. Unfortunately, I only read the one copy of the NCO that was the transcript of the telephone hearing—the one that did not include this vital information. I assumed that the two written NCOs would be identical. This would prove very problematic later.

I walked out into that cold, gloomy Saturday.

I was more distraught than I had been in years. I was exhausted, hungover, hungry, and mortified by my actions. I called my daughter Noel to come pick me up. When she arrived, I climbed into the cab of her truck. What could I tell her? Her dad had been arrested, spent the night in the Island County Jail, and then had wandered the streets of Coupeville as a broken man. It was a quiet ride home because neither of us knew what to say; we'd never been in this situation before. I made a point of contacting a good criminal attorney that weekend. Other than that, I stayed holed up in my bedroom: ashamed, hopeless, devastated. I could not rid myself of the ominous feeling of doom. My family had never seen me lose my way in life in such a devastating and dysfunctional way.

On Monday, I went to work as usual, though inside I was a totally broken person. I did tell a few trusted souls what had happened to me over the past few weeks; they were in shock, as was I.

Two days later, I went to my scheduled appointment with my lawyer. He showed me a copy of Jodi's eight-page sworn statement and I read it for the first time. I was appalled! What I read did not fit with any truths I knew. For example, she stated that we hadn't been intimate or in a relationship for over one and half years. She stated that she'd never told me where she lived. She had also formally sworn that she was scared of me, and that I had access to her personnel files at the hospital; as a board member, I was not privy to such access and she knew that, just as all hospital employees knew. After reading the long, error-filled statement, my mind went blank. How could she tell such lies, untruths that painted me in such a terrible light? Jodi even added a story about how I'd seen her and Jim at Skookum having a drink together and had followed him to his airplane hangar at the Arlington Airport. That had never happened either. I would not have stayed with Jodi if she was still seeing Jim. It made no sense to me. My mind was whirling as I finished reading her statement and saw that she had signed that the contents of her statement were true, and she'd sworn to it under penalty of perjury.

The next week was the hospital's regularly scheduled board meeting. I had attended this meeting once a month for more than eighteen years. Nobody at the hospital knew about my arrest; I was keeping the information very private. I arrived at the hospital and parked. On my way in, a dark license plate on a white car caught my attention. It was parked in the handicapped space by the front door of the hospital. I looked more closely and immediately realized it was Jim's car, the same white Buick I had seen at Jodi's house on January 1st. Jim and Jodi were both sitting in the car. I was shocked.

When Jodi saw that I had recognized them, I saw her turn to Jim and say something. He pulled out of the parking lot and drove back and forth in front of the hospital, and then drove back into the hospital parking lot and parked next to my truck. This confused me and then I began to panic; I knew I was not supposed to be within five hundred feet of Jodi, per the NCO. I decided to leave the hospital without going to the board meeting. I ran upstairs and told a fellow board member I was leaving, and then left the hospital grounds.

About half an hour after going to bed that night, I heard my front doorbell ring. There on my front porch were several policemen. They said I had violated my NCO and Jodi had contacted them. This was the first moment I learned that the NCO prohibited me from being on the hospital campus whether or not I had a board meeting there or needed medical care. Because it was Jodi's workplace, one of the NCOs (the one I had not read in my assumption that the two documents would be identical) specified that I could not be on hospital grounds. The police handcuffed me, and once more I traveled to jail handcuffed in the back of a police car. I spent a couple of hours in jail until my daughter Noel could come down with the bail money to get me out of jail. I had another sleepless night.

The Island County Superior Court contacted my attorney about my NCO violation. They were talking about revoking my release and the possibility I would be thrown back into jail without the possibility of bail. I panicked. My NCO violation hearing was scheduled for the following Monday and my attorney Lance suggested that I ask some people to attend the hearing to support me. I asked my four fellow board members, the hospital CEO, and my associate veterinarian and his wife. They all sat in the back row of the courtroom. My lawyer negotiated with the prosecuting attorney and they agreed that I should be released on bail.

It was during this time of crisis that I began to see patterns in my relationship with Jodi: non-communication after some of our extended times away is just one example. We would have a good time together exploring some new locale, and then she would be totally unavailable to get together with me for a week or so afterward; often, she'd tell me she was sick. Even when we were both home, our relationship was characterized by spending multiple nights together for a week or ten days, followed by a week or so when she was "busy" with work or family. During the latter, we would meet at a bar before she went home by six to cook dinner for her children. Another pattern I saw was that sometimes I would send text messages to Jodi and receive a string of responses from her, like having a long conversation via text message; other times, I would receive no response at all to a series of text messages over many days. This dissonance between ample time together and ample communication, contrasting with little to none of either was very disconcerting and confusing to me during our relationship. In fact, the lack of consistent communication was a source of great anxiety for me. Jodi always dismissed my concern about this, blaming me for being too sensitive. Also, I saw a pattern where, at social functions, I was not "allowed" to attend as Jodi's boyfriend, or even to acknowledge our intimate relationship in public places where we knew people. But I was trying so hard to please her, to go with what Jodi determined as the ebb and flow of our time together, and to really do whatever it took to accommodate her needs and desires.

Upon reflection, I realized that I had set out to find a wife and thought that the intimacies and trips I shared with Jodi were very possibly leading us in that direction. Jodi had been clear that her past hurts in other relationships made her a little cautious about declaring her love for me, but she also continued to engage with me intimately; to gladly receive the gifts, trips, and other monetary offerings I made; and to make remarks and have conversations that referred to an extended future together. As I looked back, I began to realize she established these patterns to accommodate both relationships. I felt like an absolute idiot.

Seven days after my second arrest, I met two friends for dinner up in Mount Vernon. I was scheduled to pick up my oldest daughter Bo Mee at the airport later that evening. She was flying in to help me, wanting to support me in my crisis. My intention was to avoid drinking while having dinner with my friends. I just wanted to visit with them. When I arrived, they each had a beer in front of them. At first, I told the waitress I did not want anything to drink. But after several minutes I decided that one beer would not hurt. I would just slowly drink it during dinner, and I'd be fine. But that beer went down easily and was soon gone; it just seemed to vanish. I was sure one more would not affect me, and I would still be able to drive the ninety minutes to the airport. I ordered a second beer. It may have been that second beer, or even the third one, when the tides inside me changed. Whatever strengths I had previously possessed to control my drinking were overcome by the pain I felt inside. I fell headlong into depression. The only recourse I knew, the one I had always turned to during sad or difficult times, was to drink. So, I did.

I drank more and more until I totally forgot about picking up my daughter. That night, I totally forgot about my duties as a father. It's not that I did not love Bo Mee and want to see her. It was just that in that instant, my love and need for alcohol was stronger. Alcohol won out. My downward spiral continued in free-fall fashion. I hoped to drink until the pain stopped, but I knew it wouldn't work. I drank until everything stopped. All reason. All consciousness. All feelings. I was in a drunken blackout stupor. It was in this condition that I set off driving on the roads of Skagit County. I was erratic enough that several people, fortunately, called the police. A sheriff found me parked off the road on a lawn. While he was watching me, I backed into a mailbox, knocked it over, and left the area totally unaware that I was being followed by a sheriff. I was arrested for the third time in three weeks in three different counties.

I was free-falling, and I didn't care. I was worn out and ragged after this January of hell. All I wanted was relief, but it wouldn't come. Death seemed like the only recourse as I sat in the back of the squad car exhausted, depressed, drunk, hopeless, and shame-filled. Jail was my destination once again. My daughters had to rescue me. Noel drove to Seattle to pick up Bo Mee, and my daughter Mariah came and bailed me out of jail. There are no events in life that have caused me more intense shame than needing my children to pick me up and bail me out of jail. It is humiliating.

I felt like the drowning victim who goes under water for the third time and never comes back up. My life had reached a bottom. I did not want to have a fourth such occurrence. I was totally worn out and used up. Completely dejected. I was done. The last twenty-eight days had ruined me. I could never again be what I once was. The brutal events of the last month had filled me with more shame than any one man can hold. I was close to my end. I was lost. I did not know what to do. I knew I had to do something to stop my rapid and continuing downward spiral.

So, for the first time in my life, I admitted I had a problem with alcohol. It had caused problems for me in the past, but never to this extent. I realized I needed professional intervention. I needed to go somewhere to stop my self-destruction. I decided to place myself into an inpatient alcohol rehabilitation center. A month before, this would have been absolutely inconceivable. Now it was an absolute necessity. I found a local rehab center with a good reputation and an immediate opening.

This was my first attempt to stop the insanity, and my first step toward sanity.

14

THE ABYSS

I was an utterly lost and broken man. Completely disoriented emotionally after the trauma of Jodi's betrayal, fueled by a month of turning to alcohol compounded by sleeplessness, I entered the recovery center. I knew I had reached the end of my run. I could go no further as I was and still survive. I felt my life could get no worse. I was not sure I could be fixed, and I was not sure I wanted to try. All I was sure of was that I wanted the pain to stop. I wanted the craziness to stop. That's why I went. I went to get away from the world. I would have traveled even farther if I could have escaped from myself. But I could not.

It was a totally strange environment and experience for me when I entered Lakeside Milam Recovery Center. I felt disjointed and afraid. I had never faced my problems with alcohol before. Alcohol had been part of my life since I took my first drink at thirteen. It was part of the fabric of my life. Alcohol had been my companion through junior high, high school, undergraduate school, veterinary school, and into my adult life. It's how I dealt with both happiness and pain. I used it to make the happy times happier and the sad times bearable. At least that's what I had told myself. Mostly, it ended the happy times earlier and prolonged the agony of the sad times. But that reality never altered my perceptions or need for alcohol. I had created problems with my drinking in the past, but they were nothing in comparison to the havoc I had wreaked over the last month. Alcohol had fueled my pain and shame into an uncontrollable, internal fire of self-destruction.

My first nights in the detox ward, I did not sleep at all. There were people coming and going at all hours. I could occasionally hear people groaning or talking nonsensically as they were recovering from whatever substance they had abused to get here. The whole atmosphere was difficult for me to comprehend. I felt so much shame. I was sixty years old and I could not fully accept that my downfall had actually occurred. I kept thinking and praying that I would wake up and find it had been a nightmare. But it wasn't. This was my life in a shambles.

On the evening of the third day, I was taking one of my walks outside. It was a cold and clear winter night. The visible vapor of my breath led me along. As I walked down the trail by the trees, one of the darkest parts of the trail, I stopped and looked up at the sky. The stars shone down on me from the immense night sky. The sheer magnitude of the sky dwarfed my body and spirit. I was already fragile and vulnerable, feeling extremely small and weak. Whatever minuscule strength and resolve I had brought to Milam left me at that moment. I felt utter panic. I realized the immensity of my undertaking. I was here to stop drinking. To quit for life. Not for a day, or a week, or one month. But for the rest of my life! I totally lost it. I was completely overwhelmed by the enormity of never drinking alcohol again in my entire life. It was unfathomable to me to not drink again. It seemed impossible. Alcohol had fueled my downfall, yet I still craved it. Anxiety flooded through my entire body. I started sweating even though it was twenty-five degrees outside. My heart raced and I felt weak throughout my body. I wanted to bolt from the campus to get away from this terror that gripped me.

But there was a tiny voice deep inside me that was almost completely drowned out by the voices of terror, shame, and pain. This tiny voice said, *You can do this, Tim. Stay the course … save yourself … people do love you.* This voice told me to call my daughter Kelly, who I felt would understand. In that call, I told her I did not think I could quit drinking for the rest of my life. I'm sure she could sense the panic and despair in my voice. Kelly said not to think of not drinking for the rest of my life; she said that I only needed to not drink for one day. I was unraveling. I told her I wasn't sure I could quit drinking for even one day. She then said to think about not drinking for twelve hours and I said even that was too long. She talked me down to six hours, then two hours, then one hour, then thirty minutes, and—finally—one minute. I rebuffed each increment as an impossible goal. Finally, Kelly said, "Dad, can you not drink for fifteen seconds?" I replied, "Yes, of course I can do fifteen seconds." So, she told me firmly and lovingly to do fifteen seconds at a time. I made a deal with her to take my sobriety fifteen seconds at a time.

One of the ways that I kept some semblance of sanity was by walking alone outside on breaks. Most of the people spent their time talking and smoking cigarettes. I walked. Every morning I would rise early and walk the perimeter of the campus. On breaks and after lunch, I would walk the perimeter of the campus. And at night, after dinner and before bedtime, I would walk the perimeter of the campus. I would walk in the rain, in the cold, in the light, and in the dark. I walked alone. I walked in silence. I walked to try to distance myself from my pain and my confusion. But I could not walk fast or far enough to leave them behind. I was lost in the confusing labyrinth of the dark recesses of my mind.

During the day, I battled my demons of alcohol addiction, which was painful and exhausting. But it was during the night that the demons arose who haunted my mind and soul. The sight of Jim naked in Jodi's closet and crawling into bed next to her appeared in my dreams on those rare moments when sleep would visit my tired body. I would awaken drenched in sweat and lie there with more questions than answers going through my head.

If I had been left alone to my own devices to face my demons, I do not think I could have succeeded. I was fortunate that during every visitors' hour at Milam, I had children, grandchildren, or good friends who would come to talk and support me. These visits helped me realize that people did care for me. They kept me from withdrawing too far into myself and my shame room. On their visits, we would walk out on the trail that I so often walked alone. I apologized for the pain I had caused them with my drinking. These were raw, emotional times for all of us. I did not take their love and support for granted. My family and friends saved me.

One week before I was scheduled to leave rehab, I called my daughter Noel to find that my world had plunged deeper into the abyss. My shame and humiliation had been made public! I had thought when I entered Lakeside that my world could get no worse, but the phone call with Noel proved it could. She was subdued when she answered the phone and told me there was something she had to tell me. There had just been a front-page article in the *Everett Herald*, the county newspaper, that detailed my three arrests and included my photo. The article chronicled my three arrests. The reporter recounted Jodi's version of events. My experience of those events was significantly different. This would all come to light in the ensuing months of court cases.

I couldn't breathe. I had that odd feeling I had prior to my onset of Bell's Palsy. I began to panic. I thought everything that could go wrong *had already* gone wrong. I was very sadly mistaken. This was clearly the end. I was sure everyone would abandon me; they would now see what a deeply flawed human piece of wreckage I was. My business had always been the stable part of my life, my place of refuge. But now the public detailing of my actions—my darkest and most shameful moments—had placed it in peril. The only thing of which I was certain was that I would need to leave Arlington if people abandoned me, because I wouldn't be able to stay in the wake of that. I wouldn't be able to stand the rejection. I had always felt a private shame. But public shame was entirely different. By its nature it is cruel. Public shame would ostracize me out of the human race. I feel I will always be branded by this shame. Ten minutes of recklessness had become my defining moments in the county paper and on the Internet.

The house I entered that bleak morning of March 2, 2016, when I returned from my twenty-eight days in Lakeside Milam was like a tomb. No person, no pet was there to greet me. It was deathly quiet. I slowly walked into the kitchen in a trance. I did not even think about turning on the heat to warm the house that had been vacant for a month with the thermostat set to fifty-two degrees. I was home. But I was not safe.

I sat down in my chair at the head of my kitchen table, the very chair I had sat in thousands of times before while eating, reading, or relaxing. The chair I had sat in during family dinners and celebrations. The chair in which I sat as I held my grandchildren on my lap. Today, though, this chair held me burdened heavy with great shame. The chair was the same, but I was not. I was crushed with pain and wracked with guilt. I was barely clinging to sanity. What I had done and what I had gone through were too much for me to fathom. I sat in that chair motionless, staring out the sliding glass door that opened into my backyard and the woods behind my home. In Lakeside I had been insulated from the world. I was now fully back in the world and had to face the harsh reality of what I had done. I felt exposed and frightened. I had lost control of my life. Both internally and externally I was in complete chaos.

The woods behind my home usually brought me a feeling of peace and tranquility as I gazed at the majestic evergreens reaching toward the sky. They brought no such feelings on this cold, dismal morning as the low clouds released their rain in a constant drizzle. The gray, foreboding sky was a harbinger of storms soon to come. My gaze was drawn to the skeletons of two tall cedar trees that had long since died but still stubbornly remained standing upright side-by-side with bare branches projecting out from their naked trunks. They were lifeless, just as I felt. I was submerged in abject despair and felt utterly hopeless.

As I sat there immersed in my pain, I began to lose the ability to discern where one problem stopped and another began. My emotional agony from Jodi's lies and betrayal, the rekindling of the pain I had never dealt with from my marriage and divorce, my immense legal issues, the public shame brought about by the newspaper article, and the emotional uncertainty as I faced my alcohol and personal problems all converged into a cavernous abyss that—in those moments in my chair—completely engulfed me. I had risked myself on love and I had lost. Now I faced the very real prospect of losing everything else: all that I had worked my entire life to achieve. I could lose my business, my friends, and the respect of the community. I could ultimately lose my freedom. I could not envision a way out of this crisis. Yet, somewhere deep inside of me I realized I needed to face it all, accepting responsibility for my life and my actions.

Time ceased to be relevant as I sat slumped in the chair. The only sound breaking the silence in the house was the baritone whisper tick-tock of the large clock hanging on the kitchen wall behind me. My entire life I had always been moving, sometimes at a frantic pace. At times, I moved in a positive direction and was rewarded with gifts such as my children, my profession, and my business. At other times, I moved in a negative direction, suffering defeats such as my divorce and problems from my drinking. At still other times, I lived close to the edge such as riding bulls, pushing my motorcycle to its limit at over one hundred twenty miles per hour, and taking other sorts of unnecessary risks.

As I sat there hour after hour, my fears spun around madly within me. I was afraid of again turning to drink to numb my pain. The acknowledgment of how alcohol had been a major factor in my demise caused an even greater fear of how continuing to drink would lead to my ultimate passing. I feared I would be alone the rest of my life. I feared for my business that I started from scratch in 1981. I feared abandonment by my family, my friends, my clients, and my community.

But my greatest fear was for my children. I wondered how my egregious actions had affected them. I considered the shame they might feel in the face of the public newspaper story. My son, Cody, told me that a co-worker told him his dad must be a sick, demented person. How much had I hurt them? Could they forgive me? I could only imagine the angst and pain I had caused my children. At that moment, a quiet prayer entered my soul. It was barely perceptible. The intentions of that prayer centered on my children. I so deeply love them. I prayed for their relief from the shame I had brought upon them. Ultimately, they are my world. They are the best of me.

These thoughts of and prayers for my children and grandchildren slowly returned me to the world of the living. I was not certain I wanted to rejoin it and doubted I possessed the strength to do so, but I realized I must try for them. I love them too much to give up on life. I called upon all the strength I could muster and slowly arose from the chair. I was cold and stiff, felt old and decrepit. I was shocked to see that three hours had elapsed as I sat in that chair. I did my utmost right then to prepare to face the harsh realities of my world.

15

CRIMINAL PROCEEDINGS

Not a day would pass that I did not have to deal with the tangled mess I had made of my life. Everywhere I would go in town, I felt people were watching and talking about me. Not a night would pass that I did not awaken in the middle of the night, drenched in a cold sweat and with a racing heart, after a vivid dream of standing at Jodi's window seeing Jim naked, or being in a dark, bottomless chasm. There was nowhere I could go to escape my actions.

Then, of course, I still had criminal charges to face: a DUI, the multiple charges related to trespassing at Jodi's, and violation of the NCO. This resulted in going to court twenty-three times over a nine-month period. Court hearings became a part of my life. To make the afternoon hearings, I would leave work by eleven thirty. Other times I would go to court early in the morning and was able to arrive at the vet clinic by nine thirty. It felt like every moment I wasn't working, I was finding, compiling, organizing, and giving to my attorney, Lance, hundreds of pages of documentation demonstrating my extensive, ongoing relationship with Jodi. These included receipts for gifts and travel, intimate text messages from Jodi, photographs of us having fun together on trips, and other intricate details about the events and logistics of being Jodi's boyfriend. I organized all of this "data" about our relationship into four two-inch, indexed binders to give to my attorney.

We also obtained copies from the hospital of the videotape on the night of my NCO arrest. This footage showed Jim and Jodi arriving in separate cars. Jim arrived first and parked. Jodi arrived ten minutes later. She drove around the entire lot, parked next to Jim, and got into his car. Never once did she go into the orthopedic clinic as she stated in her sworn written statement about the NCO violation. She and Jim had waited until my arrival on campus that fateful night and then reported my presence to the police.

I had been in rehab during February's hospital board meeting and was unable to attend the March meeting due to the NCO. The hospital CEO valued my presence on the board and so they opted to change the location of April's meeting so that I could attend without violating the NCO again (by being on the hospital premises). The meeting was moved to the Arlington City Hall. But I had an ominous feeling. I told my attorney about my concern and he drove up to City Hall to meet me thirty minutes before the meeting was to start. Ten minutes later, Jodi pulled up and parked her Boxster in plain sight directly in front of City Hall; this was so odd as she had never previously attended a board meeting. My attorney was sitting with me as we watched Jodi's arrival, and he knew I was at risk of another NCO violation. He recommended that I attend the meeting that night via telephone (instead of inside City Hall). I called in from a park bench well over five hundred feet away from Jodi's car. Jodi waited and watched the courthouse the entire time the meeting was taking place.

The multiple charges against me presented Lance and his associates with a difficult situation. Being apprehended while dressed in black and wearing a ski mask portrayed me in a very poor light. Lance discussed my case at a few professional meetings in which criminal lawyers work on case studies and defense strategies. His office spent countless hours poring over my relationship with Jodi so he could negotiate with the three different prosecutors to settle my cases with the best possible outcome.

The first case that was settled was in early August 2016 and concerned the DUI charge. Because I did not have a prior DUI, had voluntarily completed rehab, and had continued my outpatient treatment for many months, the court reduced my charge to negligent driving.

Later that same month, my trespassing case entered the sentencing phase. Based on all of the documentation I had submitted to my attorney, the prosecutor was willing to drop the felony charges and only prosecute me on the criminal trespass and vehicular prowling charges—both misdemeanors. The prosecutor still insisted on jail time and my attorney negotiated the sentence down to forty-five days (thirty days served, and fifteen days forgiven) with work release. This was a far more extreme sentence for this charge than is typical for first-time misdemeanors (which usually result in probation time rather than incarceration); even the judge and prosecutor admitted this. The prosecutor stated that it was a "rather more significant sentence than the State would normally be imposing for crimes of this nature." But Jodi had come to the hearings on several occasions and discussed her great emotional upheaval from these events; at the sentencing hearing she implored the judge in a twenty-minute prepared victim's statement to hand down a much harsher sentence than the one recommended by the prosecutor. But the judge kept it as it was. Those ten alcohol-fueled minutes I spent on Jodi's property in January of that year would cost me thirty days and nights in the county jail.

Though I was greatly afraid and dismayed about the jail time, at least I knew what I would be facing and there would be a clear endpoint to this year of extreme turmoil. After the hearing, we walked outside and Lance gave me a big hug. We were both relieved that this horrible ordeal was over. My attorney drove off to catch the ferry and I walked down to the waterfront shops. I needed to collect myself and try to process what had just transpired. I was a wreck. I sat outside by the water for thirty minutes, then I wandered down the street to the ice cream shop and ordered a double scoop of pralines and cream. It was my reward for making it through this most difficult period of my life.

I walked back up the hill to my truck and headed home. As I was crossing Deception Pass Bridge, I looked down at the beach Jodi and I had hiked on our first outing together in January 2014. It was on that beach where we had taken our first photo together as "a couple." Jodi had picked our destination that day. Even in my jumbled emotional state, I had to wryly admit to myself how apropos it was that Jodi picked "Deception Pass" as our first outing together. Indeed, it was a relationship built on her deception.

The only charge remaining was my violation of the NCO. Lance negotiated with the prosecutor, sharing the ample and unambiguous evidence that cleared me of the last charge. At last, the NCO violation charge was dismissed, and the third case was over.

Finally, after ten grueling months of pure hell, all three of my charges—in three different counties, at three different courthouses, and with three different judges—were settled. Now I had the daunting task of spending thirty days in jail and working to get my life back. It would be a long road, but I had the first step behind me.

16

SURVIVING 2016

Although my legal issues dominated my time and consumed my life during 2016, I had other issues with which I was also actively dealing that year. I was a newly declared alcoholic who was just out of a recovery center and needed to learn new life skills for coping with my disease and the pronounced stresses of life (which I'd formerly tried to assuage with drinking). I also had tremendous emotional trauma to navigate from the chaos with Jodi, the public shame of the *Herald* article, leftover baggage from my excruciating divorce years before, and a childhood and adult life that I'd never examined or processed in a therapeutic setting. Thirdly, I desperately needed the security, love, and acceptance of family and community during that terrible year: holidays, church attendance, and maintenance of my service work and commitments in my town required my attention. Finally, I needed to restore my shattered sense of well-being; I needed to reincorporate my outdoor passions and work with my hands as a wood crafter. My will to survive seemed to recognize the seriousness of my plight, and for the first time in my life I turned to other people to care for me and guide me. I knew I could not make it on my own. So, in addition to dealing with courtrooms and cases, 2016 found me deeply focused on recovery activities, therapy sessions, growing my spiritual life, engaging with family, and returning to the recreational activities that nourished my soul.

The most concrete change I had already started to make was to quit drinking. The concept of never drinking again in my life was daunting.

It was a total paradigm shift for me. Drinking had been a significant part of my life. Avoiding alcohol did not come naturally; it required hard work and ongoing—lifelong, in fact—dedication on my part. Lakeside Milam had been a good place for me to start this life change, but I realized I would need ongoing support to maintain my sobriety, especially during such a difficult and stressful time of my life.

When I left Lakeside, they recommended I continue with intensive outpatient therapy. Though I really did not want to go, I knew I could not trust my own instincts. For the next five weeks, I drove thirty-five miles through rush hour traffic after work every night to participate in three-hour-long outpatient group sessions. In addition to these five sessions per week, Lakeside required us to attend at least three outside support group meetings. After successfully navigating the initial five-week program, I attended twice-weekly sessions for eight weeks and then just once a week for another eighteen weeks. These meetings helped me stay focused on the importance of my sobriety and gave me tools to help live a full life without alcohol.

Since those initial eight months of intensive work on my sobriety, I have continued on the recovery path. The time I spend learning about how others stay sober and doing the daily spiritual practices that keep me from picking up another drink, actually replace the amount of time and energy I used to expend seeking booze. I know with absolute certainty that if I had continued on the path I was on when I turned to alcohol to dull my shame and deaden my pain, I would have totally self-destructed.

My fragile emotional state continued through much of 2016. I was in total inner chaos. For the healing of my psyche, I turned to my therapist Susan. I relied on her for guidance and strength. We had already been working together for more than a year, but she had not been able to break down all my defenses (erected over a lifetime). She had already made clear that she felt Jodi had not treated me well when we were together in 2014. For example, Susan explained that Jodi's sudden, long, and inexplicable silences were not typical behavior for people engaged in a caring relationship. She also told me repeatedly that I would be better off to stay away from Jodi. But I am a stubborn man and I was certain in my heart that if I treated Jodi kindly, with care and compassion, that she would not cheat on me. I realized how wrong I had been.

When we resumed therapy sessions in March after I got out of inpatient rehab, my emotional state was totally different. I had no secrets left. I had no pretense of strength. I felt weak and vulnerable. My pain was a raw, open wound. Susan recommended during this time of extreme emotional upheaval that we have three one-hour sessions a week. I really thought that was too often, that we would not have enough to discuss. (Just like I had lacked the desire to do the outpatient treatment after rehab, I certainly didn't want—or think I needed to—meet with a therapist thrice weekly.) But I listened to Susan and agreed to it, deferring again to professionals' judgment over my own. I soon realized she was right. It seemed like every day I was dealing with one of my legal issues or was immersed in substantial emotional repercussions from Jodi's betrayal. Susan kindly helped me survive one crisis after another that year. Most of her work really ended up being crisis management.

I felt unlovable and wondered why certain women I had loved found it so easy to lie and cheat on me. Gradually, Susan helped me realize that I had many people in my life who loved me. Every time I was ready to give up or felt totally worthless, Susan would tell me to look at how my children and grandchildren loved me, or at how my staff, clients, and community all supported me. But she also held me accountable for my part in choosing the two significantly detrimental relationships of my love life: my ex-wife and Jodi. Susan also helped me come to understand how I colluded with them in our relationships, that I shared responsibility in my dysfunctional relationships. She was also firm in making me realize that what I had done was wrong, that Jodi's actions did not make my actions right. She encouraged me to account for what I had done;

she did not let me off the hook for the wrongs I had committed. Susan cared for me when I could not. Without her guidance and support, I would not have made it.

The greatest support through this dark valley, though, came from my family. My children were unwavering in their love for me. They have been there whenever I have needed them and also at times when I did not even realize I needed them. They have shared in my public shame as my children, but they have not blamed me for it. They saw me not just as their father, but as a weak and damaged human being. They have seen me struggle in ways they had never seen before. They know what I did was wrong, but they do not think less of me; nor do they love me less. They have seen me grow as a new man from the ashes and I pray that this will make them proud of me once more.

I continued to pray for my children. Though I did not feel a spiritual connection with anyone or anything, I felt at a visceral level that some spiritual connection with God was essential for my healing. I knew I needed to turn back to the Roman Catholic church in which I was raised in order to meet my spiritual needs for sanctuary, support, and guidance. It was the church I knew, and I desperately needed familiarity that year. I attended services to hear the messages God had sent us. I went and listened for words of acceptance, responsibility, and forgiveness, all themes espoused in Christian literature, but not always lived in Christian life. I listened and heard healing words. But I always entered Mass a few minutes late and left as the last hymn was being sung so I would not have to face the congregation.

I also incorporated daily meditation into my life. I had meditated occasionally in the past, but in Lakeside I attended guided meditation sessions every morning and evening. I found this practice calmed my mind, so I continued on a nearly daily basis. Reading books on healing and reflections on the human condition helped me gain insight into myself. These books were written from a wide range of viewpoints including Christianity and Buddhism, ancient philosophy and neuroscience.

One of my greatest fears in early 2016—and the appearance of my shame-made-public in the *Everett Herald*—was that the hospital and my community would abandon me. I considered selling my vet practice and leaving town. I did not think I was strong enough to continue in Arlington. I was terrified the first day I returned to work. But my staff welcomed me back and embraced me with caring arms. They were doing all they could to protect me. My entry into rehab was a shock to them. I was their leader and I had always tried to care for them in the workplace. Now they had to care for me. They had a meeting after I entered Lakeside to figure out how to keep the clinic running in my absence. They rescheduled my appointments. They simply told clients I was taking care of family matters. They took care of me, our clients, and my business because they cared for me and the practice. They helped save me, as well as the clinic.

The moment I most dreaded was entering the exam room to see a client. But what I found in those rooms shocked and amazed me. My clients—with noticeable concern in their faces and in their voices—would ask me how I was doing. They told me they were praying for me. Many hugged me and told me they loved me. I did not know how to respond. Where I had anticipated anger and disgust, I found love and understanding. It brought me to tears over and over again.

I found similar responses at the hospital and in the community. Many people who worked at the hospital, from administrators to doctors and nurses, contacted me and voiced their support for me. Friends invited me to have breakfast with them in town. We would meet and talk about how I was doing. Other friends invited me over to their homes for dinner or cookies. I accepted their invitations even though I felt unworthy of their care and concern.

These people did not condone what I had done. However, they knew me and did not judge me solely on my aberrant behavior during that month of suffering and acting recklessly. I was mortified about what I had done, but I was met with compassion and understanding. Though I was outwardly accepted within my community upon my return from a month in inpatient rehab, I internally felt ostracized by the blatant exposure of my deeds in the newspaper article. This made it difficult for me each time I went out into public; ordinary tasks like buying groceries, attending public functions, and running errands continued to raise my anxiety.

I have always experienced a spiritual aspect to Earth and all her creatures. So, I was outside a lot during 2016. The time I spent walking in nature calmed the anxiety and voices of doom in my mind. I would look around and realize that if I lost everything, I would always find refuge in nature. Whenever I had a moment free of hearing preparations, meetings with attorneys, clinic responsibilities, therapy, or recovery work, I went hiking. I made these sojourns out into nature all by myself; I needed the respite and quiet that I knew could be mine in the natural world. These precious times I carved out of my chaotic life to spend in the solitude of the forest and mountains brought me the few small moments of peace I could muster during this tumultuous time. Often, I would find a secluded spot by a waterfall and just sit there for a while trying to relax in the mesmerizing sound of the water cascading off the mountain. Because of everything that I needed to attend to during the wreckage cleanup in 2016, these nature experiences were brief. But they were critical to my inner healing.

When the weather did not permit me to spend extended time out of doors, I went into my woodshop to find solace. Using my hands to craft projects with wood and leather has always provided me an avenue of great satisfaction and a sense of self-worth. It is a way I can retreat into my creative self and find refuge from the world. I spent many hours during 2016 in my shop working on projects for my children to help them in their businesses. It gave me a sense of purpose to be creating something out of wood that would benefit them. Focusing my mind on the wood, and the process of shaping it, afforded me a mild and temporary distraction from my emotional pain.

The continual onslaught of activities keeping me mired in my crisis did not allow for the opportunity to get out of town for more than a few hours, although I craved a change of scenery that I hoped would bring me a real break from the insanity of my life.

17

A WAKE-UP CALL TO LIFE

I have always loved the feeling of the wind as I rush headlong on a motorcycle across highways and byways. But every time I had gotten on my motorcycle during that spring of 2016—hoping for a break from my pain—thoughts of all the trips with Jodi on the back of my bike came flooding in. I became increasingly distraught. I don't know the line one must cross where suicide seems the only alternative to the endless inner turmoil and unbearable pain that can overwhelm and engulf a person. I did not cross that line but I came frighteningly close. As I rode those two-lane asphalt country roadways on my motorcycle, I could only see a past where I had acted recklessly. I could see no future. I could not forgive myself. As I took the corners too fast, I would think about how all of my problems would disappear if I went just a bit faster or a little wider. On left-hand turns, I could just go onto the shoulder into the gravel and that would end it all. All the pain and torment that engulfed me and swallowed my very soul would disappear. But visions of my family and friends kept me on the road and out of the ditches. I expressed these emotions to my therapist. I know she sensed my despair and the darkness that was ruling my life. Susan asked me not to ride, as she worried for my safety. I agreed. I was learning to heed the wisdom of others during this time of complicated crises in my life. I did not ride anymore that spring.

Several months later (in July), I told my therapist that I felt stable enough emotionally to safely ride my motorcycle. Susan reluctantly agreed and asked me to promise that I would contact her if I felt the least bit of apprehension or instability; I agreed to this. I planned to spend the weekend in eastern Washington, traveling there on my motorcycle. That day I paid more attention than usual to my riding, as I knew I was still in a fragile state. I closely monitored my speed, how fast I took corners, and my mental state. I could hear Susan's concern for my safety in the back of my mind. I shared her concern, so I took extra precautions.

As I was descending down one of the mountain passes, I came around a wide, sweeping left turn. I rode by a motorcyclist who was off his bike and pacing on the right shoulder of the road. I stopped to see if he needed help. As I approached to offer help, he kept repeating, "I can't go near the body." I asked him what he meant and he pointed to the ditch alongside the road. As I drew closer, I could see a man's body next to his Harley.

I quickly went down to him and checked for any sign of life, but I knew by his color and position that he was dead. He had no pulse. I am all too well versed in death in my profession and can sense when life is gone from a body. Once I knew for certain that he was dead, I reverently laid my hands on him, made the sign of the cross, and prayed for him. I prayed for his entry into heaven and I prayed for all those he left behind in this life. I looked at him as I knelt there and felt a great sense of loss and sadness flow over me. As I looked at him, I saw myself. He was riding alone as I often did. He was middle-aged. I imagined the family and friends he left behind and the intense sadness they would all feel when they learned of his death.

I looked up the hill and saw where he had left the road as he took that wide, sweeping left-hand corner, perhaps going too fast or perhaps just misjudging for a millisecond. That's all it took for his bike to enter the ravine and go careening through the bushes to its final landing spot. Pieces of his bike and luggage were strewn along the path where the bike had plowed through the bushes. I looked down at the man and prayed he had not suffered in his final moments. I saw how that curve in the road—the same left-hand turn that I had only two months earlier envisioned as a way out of my own despair—had taken his life in an instant. I felt the vulnerability we all face. I felt fear.

I helped as much as I could at the scene, stopping a car and sending them down to the ranger station to alert the highway patrol as there was no cell reception in this section of road. I directed traffic and tried to honor the man in his passing. I kept others away from his body to preserve his dignity and privacy. After an hour, two park rangers arrived and took over the traffic duty. Then the highway patrol arrived and I gave them my statement. I'd done everything I could in this situation. Before I left the scene, I went over to the fallen biker and offered one final prayer of farewell.

I went back to my Harley to continue on my journey. It was difficult to climb onto my bike after what I had experienced. I felt vulnerable, weak, and totally exposed. I sat on my bike for a few minutes and collected my thoughts and emotions. I knew I had no choice but to ride. I started my bike and slowly left the scene. I only rode a few miles before a flood of emotions overtook me and I had to get off my bike. I was terrified that I had considered deliberately ending my life exactly as I had just seen another human accidentally do. I thanked God he had intervened. I thanked Susan for seeing my despair and protecting me from myself. I was thankful I listened to her. I cried. Eventually, the ferocity of my emotions calmed to a level where I thought I could safely ride. I rode cautiously, with the fear of mortality my new companion. I kept alert for dangers, both real and perceived. I rode to my motel and settled in, glad to be off my motorcycle. In the past, this type of trauma would've been my excuse to drink. But on this occasion, with just a few months of sobriety under my belt, I knew I did not want to turn to alcohol. I also knew that whatever temporary dulling of emotion I might feel, it would be offset by longer-lasting pain that would remain if I did not face my emotions and deal with them. I remembered the stories of other people I'd heard talking about recovery from alcoholism and I drew strength from them in those moments. I prayed for inner strength from God to calm my soul and help me not to drink that night. He answered my prayers and gave me the strength. I did not drink.

I sent a text message to Susan telling her what I'd just witnessed and experienced. I needed someone I trusted with whom I could share my fear and sadness. I had just come face-to-face with my own mortality and vulnerability. I felt close to a total breakdown at that moment. Susan helped me settle down and reach a state where I could be with my grief. She was kind and understood how close to breaking I already was. She helped me realize that I was in shock and needed to care for myself. She told me to remember my grandchildren and to feel their love. After a fitful night's sleep, I rode back over that same highway toward home the next day. I felt a great sense of sorrow riding with me. As I passed the site of the accident, I slowed down and bid a final adieu to a fellow biker who would travel these Earthly roads no more. I thought of how those he loved and those who loved him were crying today, grieving from their sudden loss. I said a prayer for them. I wish there had been more I could have done.

I arrived home safely and had dinner that evening with one of my daughters and two of my grandchildren. I held them tight and let their love give me strength.

18

Jail

It seemed inevitable from the very outset that the result of all my actions and arrests in January of that year would be doing jail time. What wasn't clear at first was how long my incarceration would be. By August 29th, I had been sentenced to the forty-five days of which I would serve thirty. The court scheduled me to enter jail in mid-November. I would enter under work release terms, which means that I would go to my vet practice, work all day, and then spend evenings, nights, and part of the weekends locked in jail.

In mid-October, I attended an evening meeting to prepare for my jail sentence. They told me what I could bring and what to expect. I could bring no books, writing material, and not even my own toiletries. They would provide the toothbrush and toothpaste and if I wanted anything else, I would have to buy them through their dispensary. The sheriff issued a cheap, gray duffel bag to put my clothes in for my internment.

On Wednesday, November 16, 2016, at eight in the morning, I reported to the sheriff's office with my duffel bag to start my jail term. I gave him my bag so he could search it, signed some papers, and then left to go to work for the day. I had to return to the jail by six thirty every evening. Each night I parked in the lot across from the jail and walked up to the door. I pushed the button on the box near the entry. A voice came from the speaker asking me what I wanted. I replied, "Tim Cavanagh reporting for work release." I heard the metallic click of the door and he told me to come on up to the top of the stairs.

That first night I sat in a small lobby with two other work release men waiting to be let into jail. None of us spoke or made eye contact. There were small combination lockers by the door leading to the jail. One of these had been assigned to me for my keys, phone, wallet, and other personal belongings. After a short time, they unlocked the door and led us into a room where there were four more inmates waiting to be processed into the jail. One of the inmates looked at me and asked me why was there. I replied I was there on work release. He said I didn't belong there and that he thought I was a lawyer.

But I did belong there.

That night I went through the process that would be repeated every time I returned from work. The jail guards would take us into a holding area, and then each individual was led into a small room for a strip search to make sure we were not bringing in any drugs or contraband. Then the guard in the observation room would unlock the door and let me pass through; as I shut that door, I would hear a loud metallic click as the door locked behind me. I would walk down the hall through two more doors; at each one I would stop, waiting for it to be unlocked. After I passed through each door and closed it, I would hear that blaring locking mechanism. With the sound of each successive metal door being secured, I felt increasingly far from my home and the people I loved. Finally, I reached the work release section of the jail.

As I walked alone down the quiet, cold corridor, I felt a wave of exhaustion descend on me. I was emotionally, physically, and spiritually spent after enduring eleven months of pure hell as I sat through myriad court hearings. Now I faced one month in jail to end this very painful year. To punctuate my humiliation, I had to wear the jail-issued orange uniform with baggy pants and orange rubber sandals.

There were only two available beds in the freezing cold cement and metal cell. Both were on the top bunk. The jail was overcrowded and there were even people sleeping on the floor. I placed an old, thin, foam pad on the sheet of metal on the top bunk. I covered it with one of the well-worn rough sheets they gave me and used the other one under the scratchy wool blanket they provided to keep me warm. There was pillow, so I used my jacket rolled up and put inside a T-shirt as my pillow. This was to be my bed for the next thirty nights. It turned out that it was like sleeping on a rock. There was no part of my sixty-year-old body that did not hurt every day upon waking up from that cold, rigid bed.

That first night I just sat up on my bunk in the corner and tried to fathom what I had done and where I was. It was a sleepless night, as were most of my nights in jail. There was no comfortable position on the metal slab "bed," and the lights in the large common room stayed on all night. Throughout the night, sharp sounds of doors opening and shutting jolted me as the night guards came in to do rounds to check on us. The snores that emanated from my thirty-five cellmates were pervasive. Sometimes a yell would puncture through the other noises as an inmate suffered a nightmare. There were two bathrooms in the cellblock, one upstairs and one downstairs. The sound of the toilet flushing also intruded throughout the night. Add to all of these sounds my high state of anxiety; it was simply dreadful and seemingly unbearable. In addition to the physical pain, I was haunted by two recurring nightmares: my dad snapping the belt as he walked down the hallway to beat me in my bunk bed, and seeing naked Jim moving through Jodi's house and crawling into bed next to her. When these dreams came, I would wake up in a cold sweat.

At six in the morning, the guard came into the jail cell and woke us for breakfast. I got down from my bunk, stood in line, and was handed a brown paper bag with my breakfast in it. Other than the orange, the rest of the food was unidentifiable and inedible. There was a small packet of dried coffee that I mixed with lukewarm tap water from the sink for my morning coffee. It was the last jail breakfast I ever bothered trying to eat.

An hour and a half later, I changed out of my prison garb into my street clothes. At eight, I went to the locked door. I buzzed the prison guard who would remotely open the doors as I walked down the hallays, and outside into the fresh, moist, cold November air. It felt so good to be breathing clean air. I drove to work. My first stop was to an espresso stand to get a large coffee and a muffin. This was my breakfast every morning that month as I was released for work. Half an hour later, I arrived at my vet clinic to quickly shower, shave, and get dressed in my nice work clothes to start my workday by nine.

I endeavored to focus solely on the professional tasks of each day. But in the back of my mind was the awareness that I would be heading back to jail for the night. After I had finished morning surgeries each day, I would go up to my office to take a nap before my afternoon appointments started. I could not always sleep but it was nice to rest on something besides a metal bed. I would finish my afternoon appointments by quarter to six and had to be back at the jail forty-five minutes later; I absolutely could not be late returning to jail. I would fix a sandwich for dinner that I ate while driving back to jail.

My days spent working as a professional with longtime clients entrusting me with the well-being and health of their pets presented a stark dichotomy to the stark, harsh jail environment where I would spend my nights. During the day, I dressed in nice professional attire, then I would change into worn blue jeans and a T-shirt as transition clothes; I didn't want to stand out at the jail when I arrived. It felt surreal.

Sundays were especially hard because that was the only non-work-day of my week; this meant I spent the entire day in the jail in addition to the nighttime. The day passed excruciatingly slowly in jail. I divided my time between reading and writing. There was a collection of about forty paperback books that had been donated; I would try to immerse myself in any story that would take me out of the present: jail. And the writing I did was on the back of the jail request sheets that were strewn about the common room of the jail. The only writing implements were stubby, short pencils. Eventually, Monday morning would arrive when I could leave for work again. Most of my days in jail were spent thinking about where I was and what I had done to get there. In short, I contemplated my reality: at sixty years of age, I was a professional by day and—for a time—a convicted criminal at night. In Chinese traditional medicine, they talk about the root problem and the branches that arise from the root. It was easy to see the branch symptoms, but they were not the root problem. I had been pruning the branches that year and was just starting to recognize my root problem, my core issues.

Normally by midmorning on Thanksgiving, I would have my turkey prepped and ready to put in my Traeger smoker, and I would be preparing all of the side dishes. Two or three of my children and their families would have arrived to help as they savored my homemade cinnamon rolls. My kitchen would be filled with rich aromas and lots of laughter. It would be a day of love and celebration. This scene would not be played out on November 24, 2016. That day found me sitting on my top bunk in Skagit County Jail spending Thanksgiving with fellow inmates in our orange jail garb. I was very subdued and struggled to be thankful. It's difficult to count one's blessings in the eye of the storm. There are times in life when survival is a justifiable goal; that Thanksgiving Day was one of them. All day I recalled the words of encouragement my friends had offered before I started my jail sentence. Even as I deeply appreciated their attempts to comfort me, nothing felt soothing as I sat locked up, away from my loving family and friends on a holiday. Those of us in jail were bored and anxious, melancholy and dejected. A few inmates constantly paced back and forth all day long like horses without ample exercise who are kept in too-small stalls. They had blank eyes and expressionless faces. I so badly missed my children and grandchildren's hugs, laughter, and companionship. I felt like crying, I was so depressed; but I certainly could not do so in front of the other inmates. It was a very sad and lonely Thanksgiving.

When I had a week left in jail, the weight of the entire year bore down on me. That night at a quarter past two in the morning, the tears finally flowed. I could no longer hold them back. Tears filled my eyes as I lay on my back. They started draining out the corners of my eyes and down the sides of my face, wetting my wadded jacket that I used as a pillow, my clothes, and my bedding. I did not make a sound. It was a release of silent pain and despair. I slowly sat up and looked around my jail cell. I was surrounded by men, yet I felt totally isolated. I was locked away from my life. The tears came without end. I felt a depth of sadness I had never felt before for the loss of the love and dreams I had for a woman. I felt enveloping sadness about being used and feeling played like a fool. All the vulnerability of having trusted, opening my heart, and then having all of that snatched away increased my despair. I cried for my lost marriage and all the pain I and my children had experienced in the wake of that. I also felt indescribable sadness for letting my children down; I was their guide in life. But I had lost my way. I even cried that night for that little boy who had never been hugged and who was punished more severely than his actions warranted. I would carry this sadness of being a prisoner for the rest of my life. After a lifetime of denial, this sudden burst of profound sadness engulfed me. I had no one to hug me, no one to talk to. That night I had absolutely nobody. All alone, I cried. Silently, painfully, the tears cascaded down my face for twenty minutes and then they abruptly stopped. They did not cease because the sadness had lifted, but simply because the tears ran out. Spiritually, emotionally, and physically I was spent. I sat there wearing sadness like a suit. It was oppressive, but in a strange way it was also a protection against going numb. The despair, as awful and consuming as it was, at least told me that I was still alive.

My last night in jail—the night that seemed like it would never come—finally arrived. It was a sleepless one. The next day I arose early and packed everything into my gray duffel bag. I took the sheets and blankets off my bed and rolled them up. I changed out of my orange jail uniform for the last time and folded it. I went down the hallway and into the office area where I turned in my bedding and uniform, and signed the papers for my release. I had finished my jail sentence. There were those infernal locked metal doors I had passed through repeatedly over the past month. The day of my release, the guards unlocked each one as I approached. Three doors later, I passed through the last of them: out of the jail and into the freedom of the morning. I looked up into the drizzling sky and felt refreshed by the raindrops wetting my face. I imagined them washing away some of the pain from my ordeal. I was as euphoric as an exhausted man can be. I got into my truck, drove to the coffee stand one last time for coffee and a muffin. Then I drove to work.

The first night out of jail seemed so odd: I could just drive the four miles home like I had done every day for decades—until one month before. I had told my children that I just needed to be alone that night, so I could rest and recuperate. My Yorkshire terrier, Gidget, was there to greet me and she was as happy to see me as I was to see her. She has been my buddy through thick and thin. I took a very long hot shower to soothe my aching muscles and to wash away the memory of my ordeal, at least for that night. I relaxed with Gidget on the couch mindlessly watching television, but paying no attention. By eight, I knew it was time for us to go to bed. I never knew my bed could feel so good. My regular sheets felt as soft as the most expensive linens. My pillow felt like angel wings under my head. My entire body relaxed into my mattress. Sleep rapidly overtook me and I was blessed with a dreamless sleep. I thought this ordeal was over.

With only a week to prepare for Christmas after my release from jail, I was only able to sparsely decorate my house and to buy a few basic presents for the holiday. It would not be the lavish affair of years past, but it was the most heartfelt family celebration we had ever experienced. We had all suffered through the extraordinary and excruciating events of that year and we desperately needed the respite of one another's company, affection, tenderness, and conversation. The experience had brought to each of us the realization that the love of family is the most cherished gift of all.

My 2016 year through hell had finally come to an end.

19

SURVIVING, HEALING, THRIVING

I wished I had made more progress in putting my travails behind me during 2016, but that year had been much more difficult than I'd imagined. "Survival" had been my M.O. New Year 2017 was the start of a new chapter in my life. Instead of merely surviving—grunting through the anguishing emotional pain of a betrayal and breakup, drinking to excess and incurring legal repercussions, navigating courtroom hearings and culminating in a month in jail—2017, 2018, and 2019 would be years of deeper recovery and a grasp at well-being and inner peace.

One of the most important ways I continue my healing has been to maintain my sobriety. I realize that not drinking is one of the foundational pillars for my continued growth. Lakeside Milam hosts a dinner each January for alumni to celebrate recovery. It coincides with the month of my last drink. I attended in 2017, 2018, and 2019. Each time I went early and walked the perimeter on the same trail I walked so very many times when I was in rehab. These walks keep me in touch with the raw emotions I suffered during those dark days and serve as a stark reminder of the pain alcohol helped fuel. They help me stay the course. After my walks, I attend a dinner in the cafeteria and receive a coin to celebrate my continual years of sobriety.

Another pillar crucial for my recovery is my ongoing therapy with Susan. She helped me through the brutality of 2016, but we both realized that I had much more to learn about myself in order to grow from the mess I had made of my life. It was a slow, arduous process and it was difficult at times for me to detect actual change. The best markers of change inside me came in different ways—sometimes very succinct thoughts that would come to me, sometimes in dreams, and sometimes very noticeable emotions would descend on me.

In early 2017, the first of these "markers" came to me as I was walking across my bedroom floor in the early morning. A very clear, soothing voice simply stated, *Tim, you are not evil.* That was all. The words stuck with me. I was not evil. It was the beginning of a major internal paradigm shift.

The dreams that visited me at night changed over time. I had been having recurring nightmares about Jim over at Jodi's, as well as those nights I had spent in jail. Slowly, these were replaced by more positive dreams. The first was in late spring. It was a dream of a family reunion in the Colorado mountains. My entire family was there, as was Jodi—but she just stood to the side and never moved. My oldest brother came up and put his hand on my shoulder, saying, "You will be okay, Tim. You are on the right path. Keep doing what you are doing." I awoke feeling certain I *was* on the right path.

Later in 2017, I had another powerful dream. In this dream, I had fallen madly in love with a woman I did not truly know. I realized this was the pattern that had put me in such peril with the two women who had hurt me in adulthood. I told her I could not give her all my love so quickly. I reached out and she handed back to me a small gold box which contained my most precious love. I had bestowed this treasure on her much too rapidly when our relationship started. I told her she would have to earn my love, as I would need to earn hers. Love requires work, honesty, and caring. Real love is not easy, but it is the most valuable of possessions.

Just as my nighttime dreams changed, I could also feel moments of emotional change during the day. The most palpable change was with my children and our family gatherings. We have always been close and enjoyed times together, but now we were even closer and valued our family ties more than ever. We had shared my trauma as a family. My children saw me moving forward in a positive direction and our family connections grew even stronger. We felt this most powerfully during our holidays, especially the first Thanksgiving we were all together—a year after I had spent that holiday in jail, away from my children. There was a particularly special moment I felt during that holiday. I went upstairs to see my grandchildren playing in the large playroom. As I entered—hearing the laughter of children upstairs and the gaiety of adults downstairs, I felt a sea change come over me. I was surrounded by laughter, yet inside of me I experienced absolute quiet. I felt a peace I have never felt before. There were no inner voices of doubt, blame, or shame. There was only a gentle feeling of love and compassion. For the briefest of moments, I was suspended in time, knowing I was exactly where I was supposed to be. I relished that profound calm. I carry that moment with me as evidence that I am changing.

An equally important pillar of recovery is the work I do to find my spiritual connection in life. I follow the traditional route of staying connected to an organized religion, in my case the Catholic Church. But I feel there is much more to spirituality than church. I find it in the world around me—in nature, in my work, and in others. I spend time every day in quiet meditation to allow me to fully experience my life as a spiritual being.

As much as I made positive progress in my life, I still faced significant issues. The first one came in the form of a subpoena served on me at my clinic in April 2017. Jodi was suing me in a civil lawsuit for retaliation, infliction of emotional distress, and invasion of privacy. She was also suing the hospital for sexual discrimination, seeking monetary damages from both the hospital and me. She stated I was acting in my role as Chairman of the Board when I went to her house and then broke the

NCO. I realized I needed a good attorney. I was referred to a lawyer in Lynnwood who read Jodi's statement to the judge and said it looked very bad for me; his firm was not large enough to represent me adequately. He referred me to a prominent attorney in Seattle. She came hopping into her large conference room on one foot, a heel having just broken off one of her shoes. After she sat down and read Jodi's statement, she said I would lose the case and it was only a matter of how much money Jodi would get. I tried to explain that Jodi's statement was full of lies. But the lawyer kept brushing off my comments. She said that because I had been convicted, I would lose. I felt totally dejected after having two lawyers tell me I would lose this case, no matter what the whole truth was.

Shortly after that meeting, I was contacted by the claims adjuster for the insurance company representing the hospital. They had arranged for me to meet with an attorney in Lynnwood about my case. When I arrived in Eric's office just after lunch, I was prepared for bleak news. I was sure that the attorney and the claims manager (who was also there) would say that my side of the story was unimportant. I sat down, and we made small talk for a few minutes. Then they both turned to me and asked me to explain my side of the story. Over the course of the next four and a half hours, I described in detail my relationship with Jodi, what I had seen on New Year's 2016 through her window, and the subsequent month of reckless behavior that led to my downfall. I recounted my time in rehab and jail. I told them about my ongoing work in therapy to heal and learn from my mistakes. Eventually, the claims manager left to catch the ferry home. I stayed and talked to Eric until six thirty. He listened intently, taking notes and asking questions. He exuded a calmness and a caring persona that put me at ease. He told me that he understood my actions, even though what I did was wrong and illegal. At the end of our lengthy conversation, he bluntly asked me, "Do you think Jodi deserves any money?"

I replied, "Hell no!"

He simply responded, "Then we'll take this to trial if we need to."

I knew Eric was the lawyer for me. Over the ensuing months, I made many more trips to Eric's office where we would pore over all the evidence in my four notebooks outlining my relationship with Jodi, her relationship with Jim, and his relationship with his wife and two children in Montana. We spent one entire afternoon analyzing the hospital surveillance camera videos showing Jim and Jodi's activity the night I was arrested for breaking the NCO. Eric also came up to my area twice. Once we went to the hospital and retraced the occurrences of my arrest. Afterward, we went to downtown Arlington where I showed him the place Jodi had parked in front of the courthouse to try to have me arrested again.

The second time Eric came up to my area, we went to Stanwood to visit her house; I was not in violation of the NCO because she had already moved away and no longer owned that house. Eric wanted to see the window I'd looked in. He was interested in seeing if it was physically possible for me to reach in without knocking off all the decorative items on the inside of the windowsill; this is one of the many things Jodi had said I'd done but which was untrue. My attorney also went over and talked to Jodi's next-door neighbor. This man told Eric that he assumed Jim was on the title of the house because he was there on a regular basis, had never been absent for any prolonged period of time, and that Jim had often attended the HOA meetings. When we left, I showed Eric the pasture overlooking the Sound where Jodi had declared we should build our house; Eric documented this with photographs. For the next few months, he worked to prepare my case.

Feeling the need for the familiarity and comfort of family during this turbulent time, I drove home to Colorado that summer with my dog, Gidget. It would be the first time I had seen my family of origin since my arrests. I went to see my mom who had severe dementia and was in a special care home. I visited her three days in a row. She never remembered I had been there the previous day. It was sad. I could tell her condition had deteriorated significantly. She had a thirty-second attention span. She just kept asking how many children I had. I would say, "Six."

"That's a lot of kids," she would reply. Then she would ask me again how many children I had. I told her I loved her and then she would sit quietly for a while. She was frail. I wanted to give her a bear hug like when I was a small boy, but I realized it would crush her. I hoped my mom could feel my love for her.

I just sat with her, holding those weak, bony, cool hands in mine. These were the hands that had baked me bread and cinnamon rolls. These were the hands that had sewn my clothes, darned my socks, and patched my old blue jeans. These were the hands that cleaned my home and washed my clothes. These were the hands I held. My mother's hands. I sat there until she told me it was time for me to go. I so wanted to talk to her, but there was no one to talk to. I told her again that I loved her and gave her a gentle hug. She didn't actually hug me back. She looked at me with a look I remembered from my childhood when I was in trouble and she said, "Try to stay out of trouble for once." I just smiled, saying that I would. As I walked out, I told her once more that I loved her.

As I left her that July morning and walked across the parking lot to my truck, I thought that it probably would be the last time I would see my mom on this Earth. I was sad that I hadn't been able to carry on a meaningful conversation with her in years. I had desperately wanted to talk to her about my childhood and our family: how she felt about raising eight children with ofttimes such great economic constraint, whether she had enjoyed us or loved us. I wanted to know about her life and who she was. I wondered if she had been happy and what her fondest memories were. But these had all been taken from her, erased. So, we couldn't talk. She couldn't shed light on her life or my life. She was gone in mind and spirit. Indeed, my premonition was correct, it was less than two months later when my mom's body died; sadly, her mind had gone years before.

I was dismayed that I had never known my parents as people. My dad never dropped his guise as the all-knowing patriarch of the clan. He continued to rule his boys with an iron fist. He never once was vulnerable with me. I never knew his fears or frailties. We never talked as equals. I think he respected me, but it was difficult to gauge. I tried one time to ask my dad about his childhood and his parents, but I was quickly rebuffed. I wanted to know if he was happy about having us kids, as I knew it had been difficult. But I never felt I could talk to him about such personal things. I wanted to know and understand him as a person, a human being. But that never happened. I loved my dad, but I never knew him.

While I was back in Colorado, I took a day and visited the places that were important in my youth. I visited our first home. I visited the hills I had roamed and the farms I worked. All of these open spaces had been turned into housing developments and golf courses. I felt the need to visit the site of my first drink, a friend's single-wide trailer. That was gone, replaced by a new home with a van parked in the driveway. Everything was different.

I drove up into the mountains to join my brothers, sister, nephews, and nieces for a few days of camping and companionship. This was my first time back as a sober man. Everyone accepted this new part of me and embraced the change. It was great spending time with my family. We did not discuss my problems. Our time together was an opportunity to celebrate the love of family.

In October 2017, my attorney sent questions to Jodi's lawyer for her to answer. In these questions, he probed into her relationship with Jim and requested all communications between them. Jim had opened himself up as a focus of Eric's investigation because he was an active participant in setting me up for my second arrest. Eric meticulously crafted the questions to extract the truth from Jodi and expose her duplicity. I had received similar questions from her attorney and had sent my responses back in a timely fashion. But after Eric submitted these inquiries for Jodi's response, all communication stopped. We waited for Jodi to respond. We waited, and then waited some more. Seven months passed with absolutely no response from Jodi or her attorneys.

With this lawsuit still hanging over my head, a constant reminder of my painful recent past, I continued my life as a father, veterinarian, community member, and as a hospital board member. As much as I felt self-conscious in public after the newspaper articles, I continued my duties, hoping in time that this entire episode would come to an end. I realized I had to move forward and could not hide if I wanted my life to improve.

In November 2017, my term on the hospital board expired; I had to run for reelection. Being on the board is important to me, it is a way I give back to the community that has been so good to me. I realized putting up election signs would remind people of the newspaper articles and what I had done. Indeed, some people were outraged I was running. Friends would tell me they had heard people make snide comments, such as, "How could he even be around after what he did?" One lady was so infuriated that she went to both the city hall and county courthouse demanding that I be removed from the ballot. In spite of this lingering sentiment, I won the election, receiving over seventy percent of the vote. I was relieved, and realized that the majority of people in my community supported me. This was a very important moment for me in terms of still feeling accepted by my community.

In late May 2018, I met with Eric and we decided it was time to contact Jodi's attorneys. Eric called her attorney but did not hear back from her. He drafted a carefully worded letter in which he laid out the advantages of Jodi dropping the suit. He also offered my forgiveness of the eighteen-hundred-dollar loan that I had made to Jodi for a new washer and dryer. But he did state that I wanted her to return the motorcycle riding gear that I'd loaned to her. Two and a half months passed with no response. In mid-August I received an early birthday present in the form of an email from Eric; Jodi's lawyers had just filed notice with the Island County Court that, effective August 27, 2018, they would no longer be representing Jodi in her civil lawsuit against the hospital and me. In early September, Eric sent a letter directly to Jodi with a proposed court order to dismiss the suit. Again, there was absolutely no response. Eric sent another letter to Jodi about six weeks later, setting up a date to call her at her work for a discovery conference. On the designated day, Eric called Jodi's work number. The receptionist told Eric that Jodi had called in sick that morning. About two weeks after that, Eric sent Jodi one last letter giving her the opportunity to respond. Once again, on the designated day for their call, Jodi was not at work.

After being rebuffed twice, Eric had no choice but to file a notice in the Coupeville court to compel Jodi to respond. He simply wanted her to sign the papers to drop the lawsuit. Finally, Jodi signed the papers dropping the lawsuit in mid-March 2019. She neither repaid the money she owed me, nor returned my motorcycle gear. But I did not care. After two years, the lawsuit was over. The final formality was to bring it up at the April board meeting, as the hospital was a co-defendant. On the agenda, it appeared simply as, "Update on Lawsuit Against District." I was silent and hung my head as the CEO informed the other board members that the suit had been dropped. When I left the boardroom, I reflected on how it had been the April board meeting three years prior that Jodi had parked and waited in front of City Hall to have me arrested again. On this night, I felt I was finally getting free of that terrible time in my life and all the misery it had brought.

Amidst the pressure of the civil suit, I had turned to the mountains (as I have always done for solace). I chose Mount Rainier as my first big climb and selected a reputable guide company to get me there. I started training three months prior to the climb to get in shape. But no sooner had I settled into my exercise schedule when one of my veterinarians left. This increased my already full workload by twenty-five percent and included working Saturdays. I had also started a clinic remodel. I was just too tired to get in all the training I needed.

In early May, I drove to Ashford. We gathered in the morning for orientation. Our head guide was Eric, who would be teaching us mountaineering skills and ensuring our safety on the mountain along with other guides: Jenny, Lydia, James, and Nick. I came to respect the mountain guides as world-class athletes. They climb mountains on a daily basis that most of us consider a once-in-a-lifetime endeavor. At night, they provide meals for the climbers. That day they went through our equipment and we learned which knots and basic climbing techniques to use. The next morning, we were driven to Paradise, a small village at the base of Mount Rainier. We geared up and started the forty-six-hundred-eighty-foot climb up to Camp Muir, which sits at an elevation slightly above ten thousand feet. We stayed in a small hut for the next three nights. I felt fatigued the last thousand feet, but made it with encouragement from James telling me I could do it.

The first day on the mountain, we learned climbing skills such as setting anchors, ice-ax arrests, and rappelling. The second day we traversed the Cowlitz Glacier and climbed up to the Ingraham Flats at about eleven thousand two hundred feet. I was a little tired but not exhausted. We set anchors and, one at a time, we were lowered into a giant crevasse so our team members could "rescue" us. When my turn came, I was lowered down twenty-five feet and dangled from the ropes for fifteen minutes. It was unnerving at first. I could only see massive walls of ice surrounding me. Three words kept running through my mind: "beautiful, peaceful, terrifying." We climbed back to Camp Muir and received instructions from the guides for the next day's summit attempt, and then climbed into our sleeping bags to get a few hours of sleep.

We arose at one thirty in the morning to prepare for our ascent up the mountain. We had an hour to don our climbing gear—base layer of clothes; transponders in case of emergency; climbing harness complete with carabiners and cords; climbing helmet with headlamp attached; and a large pack containing water, food, and spare clothing. A quick cup of instant coffee and a freeze-dried meal of eggs and hash fueled me for the climb. We worked quietly and diligently, each lost in our own thoughts.

Then we gathered outside our bunkhouse and were given last-minute instructions, clamped our crampons onto our hard snow boots, and roped up. The air was cool and still, the darkness of the black sky was decorated by the night's display of bright stars—a perfect night to undertake the challenge of Mount Rainier at fourteen thousand four hundred and ten feet. I was in the second group with our guide, James. We set off at a slow, steady pace over the frozen glacier snow, which crunched sharply under our hard boots and sparkled like diamonds when the crystals were illuminated by our headlamps.

Rhythm. Pace. Balance. Breath. All are essential for a successful climb, yet none of these seemed to be in my skill set on this early morning. The first quarter mile was fine, but I was not walking smoothly and efficiently. By the next quarter mile, my breathing became labored, and my muscles started to ache—especially my hips and thighs. It required conscious effort to make them continue to move. Once we were into the steep, loose, exposed rock fields, I was in a total struggle. The realization that the summit would not be my destination descended over me.

My goal became making it to Ingraham Flats where we had hiked the day before (for crevasse training). I arrived there again, exhausted. I knew that eleven thousand two hundred feet would mark the highest point of my climb. I called it: no more for me. I could go no farther. I shuffled into the break barely able to pick up my feet and place them even six inches in front of me. I desperately wanted to stop short of our break area, but James commanded me on. "You can't stop here, Tim. You have to move on." Once there, I dropped my pack and pulled out my parka so I would not become chilled after perspiring from my exertion. I sat on my pack, having spent all my energy; my hopes of summiting were crushed.

Physical failure does not come naturally to me and I do not handle it gracefully. But I had no choice. My body had carried me as far as it was capable. Had I failed? Had all of the emotional and spiritual work I had done over the last two and a half years changed me enough that I could accept this as a disappointment, or would this be a devastating event? Which way would I go? My mind was trying to figure out how to frame the fact that I would not summit. Slowly, my breathing returned almost to normal and my aches began to subside a bit. There were two other climbers who had also "hit the wall"; they would be returning with me to basecamp. We sat there and watched as the other climbers slowly ascended the glacier toward the summit. Lydia, one of the guides, stayed with us to lead us back to basecamp. We were all silent, lost in our own thoughts and disappointments. As I sat there on the glacier field, I looked up into the infinite coal black sky. Stars were everywhere. Stars stacked on stars leading to galaxies millions of miles away. The Big Dipper was perched just above Mount Rainier, marking for me my True North. That's the moment I found peace with my decision to not summit. There was no noise, save the regular breathing of my companions. There was no breeze and no sound for it to carry. There was only calm. My entire world at that moment was that glacier field, my two companions, our guide Lydia and the beautiful and indescribable immensity of the night sky. My world was calm, and that calmness enveloped me. I sat on that glacier disappointed but okay with myself. I had not failed, and I was not a failure. I had chosen to be disappointed but not devastated. I realized that although my summit would not be that day, my trip and time on the mountain was time well spent.

Finally, the time came for us to pack up and trek back to Muir. It was a quiet trip down. We arrived in camp around five in the morning. The three of us watched the sun as it painted the clouds hanging over the Cascade Mountains a deep vivid orange. We stood in silence and then walked back to our bunks to try to catch the sleep that had eluded us early in the morning. I had seen amazing sunrises and sunsets. My world for those days was the mountain. I had felt the healing touch of Rainier. My dream was to return.

I realized how vital the mountains are to my emotional, spiritual, and physical well-being. In the mountains, I found both peace and challenge. I wanted to try Mount Rainier again, so the following year I signed up for three climbs with the same company; the final one would be another summit attempt on Mount Rainier in late August. I undertook the challenge of the mountain with a new respect. I started working out five times a week, doing both cardio and strength training. I also climbed many of the more demanding peaks in western Washington on the weekends: Mailbox, Mount Si, Granite Mountain, Mount Dickerman, Mount Pugh, Lookout Mountain, and Hannegan Peak. I did three good climbs in early spring to prepare for my first big adventure in Alaska.

In early May, I flew to Anchorage to spend ten days on the glaciers at the base of Denali. At the airport, I met up with our guides, Hannah, Luke, and Lucas, along with the seven other climbers in the group. From there we drove to Talkeetna and the next day were flown in a small ski plane and landed on the glaciers. When I disembarked from the plane, I was struck by the sheer magnitude of the glaciers and the mountains. They were awe-inspiring. I was blessed to be spending the next ten days exploring their grandeur. I was also blessed to spend the time with a wonderful group of people. Hannah was the lead guide, and she was assisted by Luke and Lucas. They took great care of us. We camped on the glacier, moving camp every few days. This entailed walking on snowshoes carrying a forty-pound pack and pulling a sled weighing thirty-five pounds. During the daytime, we practiced glacier travel, hanging in crevasses, and snowshoeing up mountain ridges. We would eat lunch on the surrounding mountain peaks. On two of the days, snowstorms made visibility almost zero, and we stayed in camp to work on rescue systems and knots. There was daylight twenty-four hours a day. The nights were especially beautiful. I would get up in the middle of the night and stand outside all alone, the silence broken by occasional avalanches on the surrounding mountains. The world at that hour was bathed in a blue-hued light that made Denali and the entire range seem even more mystical.

I soaked in the tranquility of these times of solitude. All too soon, my Alaska adventure came to an end and I returned home.

I continued my workouts and weekend hikes until mid-July, when I went on a four-day hike and climb into the Glacier Peak Wilderness Area to climb Glacier Peak. It is the fifth tallest mountain in Washington, with an elevation of ten thousand five hundred forty-one feet and I felt it was a good warm-up for Mount Rainier. I met Andy, the lead guide; his assistants, Grayson and Cal; and my fellow climbers at the ranger station in Darrington. After a basic gear check, we drove to the trailhead. The first day, we hiked nine miles into the wilderness area carrying fifty-five-pound packs, and set up our first camp. The mountain was ablaze with colorful wildflowers in the open meadows. The weather was perfect. On the second day, we hiked six miles and set up camp by a beautiful small lake in view of Glacier Peak. Just after one in the morning, we woke up and readied ourselves for an alpine ascent. The wind was howling as we hiked four miles by the light of our headlamps over rocks and through streams to reach the mountain glacier: the start of the climb. We summited just as the sun was rising over the eastern mountain ranges. It was an awesome sight as the sun increasingly illuminated the mountains that surrounded us. We celebrated our summit, then headed back to camp, reaching it twelve hours after we had left. After resting for an hour, we packed up our gear and hiked back to our first campsite. After one final night out under the stars, we awoke early on the last day and hiked back to our vehicles. We had our celebratory meal back in Darrington. Andy and Grayson presented me with a summit certificate. Unfortunately, Cal had to take a climber back and was not with us. I spent two hours enjoying the company of my fellow climbers.

As I drove home that day, I felt I was ready for my second attempt up Mount Rainier—just a month away. I had three climbs planned before then to ensure I was in the best possible shape. Whatever happened on Mount Rainier, I had already spent a magnificent summer in the mountains stretching from Alaska to Washington.

EPILOGUE

Three years had passed since my downfall in January 2016 and two years since I had finished my jail sentence. I had made major changes in my life. I celebrated my third year of sobriety on January 27, 2019. Where once I could not visualize my life without drinking, now I fully embraced an alcohol-free life. I was finding peace with myself. I had come to understand my reckless acts that January as the actions of a hurt and desperate man. That did not justify what I did that night, but I was finally starting to learn to forgive myself and move on.

I had turned to the mountains as a place to heal. I cherished the solitude and beauty they afforded me, but I also embraced the challenge they held. It was this challenge that brought me back to Mount Rainier in late August 2019 to attempt another summit. I was apprehensive after my previous failed attempt. I met my climbing guides and fellow climbers on the 25th of August, my sixty-fourth birthday. That day the guides, Pete, Matias, and David, carefully checked our gear. The next day, we hiked to a snowfield and practiced glacier travel and safety techniques.

On the following morning, we started our climb from Paradise at the base of the mountain. It was a perfect day, and the mountain was bathed in sunlight. For the first two thousand feet, we walked on well-developed trails that we shared with a myriad of other hikers and climbers. Then we left the trail and entered the Muir Snowfield, leaving most of those other hikers behind. After climbing another two thousand feet, we reached the ten-thousand-foot elevation of Camp Muir, where we spent the night. I arrived feeling good and looked forward to the actual climb the next day. Our initial plan was to start the climb at one in the morning the following night, a typical alpine summit. But the next morning, our lead guide told us that because of the good weather, we would start our ascent in the early afternoon in hopes of reaching the summit at sunset. Weather in the mountains can change rapidly and he wanted to take advantage of this window.

We spent the morning readying our equipment. At one thirty in the afternoon, we roped up in our teams and set out. I was in the first group, roped in behind Pete. It took just slightly over an hour to cross the Cowlitz Glacier up to Ingraham Flats (over eleven thousand feet) where we took our first break. This was as far as I had gotten on my previous climb. On that early morning, I had arrived totally exhausted. But on this second attempt, I arrived at Ingraham Flats feeling good, and not even winded. The next eleven hundred feet of the climb took us straight up Ingraham Glacier and Disappointment Cleaver: a steep, rough climb over an exposed rock field. We took another break; this was the last opportunity to turn back if a climber felt they could not continue. I felt good and only slightly tired, so I committed to the summit: more than twenty-one hundred additional feet across glaciers. Over the next two and a half hours we climbed, at one point climbing up a thirty-five-foot aluminum ladder to cross a large crevasse. The continual push forward started wearing on my energy and, as I approached the summit, I had to draw on my inner strength to keep moving. I remembered my conversation with my daughter Kelly about not drinking for fifteen-second intervals; I knew I could keep climbing for fifteen seconds at a time, so I did.

Finally, the summit came into sight. The wind was blowing and cold as we reached the rim of the dormant volcano. I felt elated! I had made it. I looked down into the snow-filled crater and felt a sense of accomplishment. Columbia Crest, at fourteen thousand four hundred and ten feet, is the tallest point in the state of Washington and sat just on the far side of the crater. The final leg of my journey took me across the crater and soon I was standing on top of the Crest just as the sun was starting to set. At that moment, I felt like I was standing on top of the world. An immense vista spread out below me in every direction.

After twenty minutes enjoying the summit, the time came to descend. Our climb was only half done. There is a saying that each of my guides has instilled in me: "To summit is optional, to descend is mandatory." We started down the glacier as the sun was setting. Mount Rainier's triangular shadow extended east over the mountain ranges as far as I could see. Our descent went smoothly, and we arrived back into camp at eleven thirty at night. I was exhausted, yet also exhilarated. After a light dinner, I crawled into my sleeping bag and fell instantly asleep.

At three in the morning, I awoke. I wanted to go outside, as one of my favorite moments in the mountains is in the early morning hours when no one else is awake. These quiet moments let me reflect on my life and soak in the tranquility of nature. A light mist hung in the air and very fine raindrops were starting to fall. There were lightning storms I could see on the western horizon. I simply stood on the mountain letting nature's gentleness soothe me. It was at that very moment, as I looked down at the lights of Paradise softened by the light drizzle, that a voice came to me. It gently and kindly said, *I'm proud of you, Tim.* The voice said no more, as there was no more to say.

A warmth slowly swelled inside of me, emanating from the very core of my body. At that moment I felt a total peace and acceptance. The softest, gentlest of tears formed in my eyes and slowly flowed down my face, mixing with the drizzle. I softly cried. I had made it. Not only to the mountain summit on this climb, but also through the harsh ordeals of my life, especially the last three years, which had been extremely brutal and cast me into the darkest moments of my life. For twenty minutes I stood there, relishing this precious moment, and then exhaustion once more called me to sleep.

Later that morning, we packed our gear, climbed down to Paradise, and drove to Ashford for our celebratory meal and drinks—an iced tea for me. Pete, Matias, and David congratulated each of us and presented certificates for summiting. We talked for an hour about the mountains, as well as past and future climbs. I greatly enjoyed this camaraderie with the guides and fellow climbers. Then the time came for me to leave.

The four-hour drive home gave me time to reflect on the climb and the road my life had taken. I realized it had been *exactly* three years before—August 29, 2016, at two in the afternoon—when I was sitting at the defendant table in the Coupeville courtroom listening for twenty minutes as Jodi vilified me, imploring the judge to impose a longer jail sentence for my heinous crimes against her. Today—August 29, 2019 at two in the afternoon—I sat at a picnic table in Ashford listening to all the guides congratulating me on my successful climb and discussing future climbs. These events could not have been more diametrically opposed: one of the darkest hours of my life and one of the brightest hours of my life.

I came to realize that all of my hard work had paid off. Physically, all of the hours spent working out and all the training climbs had propelled me to reach the summit of Mount Rainier. Even more importantly, the countless hours I had spent in therapy, working on this book, and time spent with family and friends had propelled me to an "emotional" summit. I hope these two summits will be the first of more to come as I continue working to improve myself.

I came to understand that my time with Jodi had destroyed my life, leaving it in a pile of rubble. I had been at a crossroads. I could have just buried the pain and returned to my old life. It would have been the easiest route and I might still have found a decent life in it. But I chose to build a better life out of the rubble. I did not have to remain the person I had become through life, much of it characterized by those survival mechanisms I had used throughout my youth and adulthood. Now I could draw from the wisdom of others, as well as finding my own inner compass, to actively make changes to become a more whole person.

I felt I was learning to journey well on life's rocky trails.

DENALI

I journey to these mountains,
To feel her healing touch.
I invite her grandeur to me,
For the peace I yearn so much.

I do not come to conquer her,
Just to scale her mighty peaks.
For men that feel superior,
It is a tragic end they meet.

I come to see her beauty,
In her peaks that hold the sky.
And in her snow-filled valleys,
Each bring awe to my eye.

I listen to her talk to me,
In the stillness of the night.
And in the roar of avalanches,
That remind me of her might.

I am honored she invited me,
To spend time in her land.
The longer the mountains cradle me,
It is me I understand.

I am a part of nature,
I do not stand alone.
I feel the peace inside of me,
In these mountains I call home.

CPSIA information can be obtained
at www.ICGtesting.com
Printed in the USA
FSHW011802280920
74178FS